FROM DATA TO PUBLIC POLICY

Affirmative Action, Sexual Harrassment, Domestic Violence and Social Welfare

Edited by
Rita J. Simon

Women's Freedom Network
&
University Press of America, Inc.
Lanham • New York • London

Copyright © 1996 by
Women's Freedom Network
University Press of America,® Inc.
4720 Boston Way
Lanham, Maryland 20706

3 Henrietta Street
London, WC2E 8LU England

Copublished by arrangement with the Women's Freedom Network

Library of Congress Cataloging-in-Publication Data

From data to public policy : affirmative action, sexual harrassment,
domestic violence, and social welfare / edited by Rita J. Simon.
p. cm.
Includes bibliographical references.
1. Policy sciences. 2. Social policy. 3. Affirmative action programs.
4. Sexual harassment. 5. Family violence. 6. Sex role. I. Simon,
Rita James.
H97.F76 1996 361.973--dc20 96-41460 CIP

ISBN 0-7618-0524-9 (cloth: alk. ppr.)
ISBN 0-7618-0525-7 (pbk: alk. ppr.)

TABLE OF CONTENTS

Introduction

Five major themes, affirmative action, sexual harassment, domestic violence, welfare reform, and the use of data to shed light on public policy issues, are addressed and analyzed in this second volume based on papers presented at the 1995 Women's Freedom Network National Conference. Founded in 1993, the Women's Freedom Network supporters and contributors now number about 700 men and women from all parts of the country. They range in age from their early twenties to their mid sixties. Many are academics. Lawyers and other professionals are also well-represented, as are business people and full-time mothers and homemakers. The Women's Freedom Network views women as competent, responsible individuals who do not need to have standards lowered for them to be able to compete effectively for jobs or to gain acceptance into institutions of higher education. It believes that one standard of excellence should prevail for both men and women. The Women's Freedom Network respects careful research and objective interpretations of data derived from well-designed studies and accurate reporting of the results.

In the first section of this volume, two economists and an entrepreneur examine the impact of affirmative action that focuses on the equality of results for women in particular, and for society as a whole. Sally Pipes, President of the Pacific Research Institute, argues that the fundamental problem with equality of results based affirmative action is that it assumes free individuals left to their own devices will not manage their own lives in a way that promotes their general welfare. Partisans of equality of results, she continues, believe we need so-called enlightened social planning. Pipes cites public opinion polls and the California Civil Rights Initiative that would end all race and gender based decisions in California's public sector as having popular support. She also cites studies showing that the gender gap has almost closed between men and women when years in the workplace, education levels, and marital status are controlled. Currently there are 7.7 million women-owned businesses in the U.S. generating $1.4 billion in sales and employing more than 15 million people.

Deborah Walker argues that affirmative action equality of results legislation, designed to give women special treatment is both economically unsound and detrimental to women. Walker is an economist on the faculty of Loyola University in New Orleans. In her review of the history of affirmative action since its birth in the 1960s, she demonstrates how it has been reinterpreted from its original focus of providing equality of opportunity to equality demanding results. Walker argues that some of the unintended consequences of affirmative action are an increase in sexism, a decrease in productivity, and an increase in bureaucracy, none of which are desirable social goals.

Based on her experiences, and in her role as an entrepreneur and President of the Artkraft Strauss Sign Corporation, Tama Starr takes us through the mind-boggling task of operationalizing affirmative action goals at a micro-level. She does so by providing us with a step by step analysis of a typical contract a business firm is likely to receive from a local, state, or federal agency, with its directives about how affirmative action goals have to be implemented. The costs in time, money, and brain damage are enormous.

The second theme, sexual harassment, like affirmative action has its roots in the 1964 Civil Rights Act. UCLA Law Professor Eugene Volokh traces the history of the concept of sexual harassment in the courts from the early *quid pro quo* sexual extortion definition, e.g. "Sleep with me or I'll fire you," to the hostile work environment interpretation. Citing cases such as that of Graydon Snyder, a professor at the University of Chicago Theological Seminary, and a report by the AAUW which defines harassment to cover anyone who even once in high school has been the target of an unwanted sexual comment, joke, gesture or look, Volokh shows that with each passing year, the concept of sexual harassment has become increasingly vague, and has been interpreted more broadly. Today it poses serious free speech problems, and risks, in Volokh's opinion, "crushing innocents and cheapening the coin of the harassment allegation."

Free-lance journalist and Vice President of Women's Freedom Network Cathy Young, also assesses the impact of recent sexual harassment decisions and warns that "the current sexual harassment orthodoxy leads to a far-reaching effort to sanitize the workplace in ways that may make the work environment more hostile." By way of examples, she shows how it polarizes the sexes and sets up different standards for men and women. It suppresses sexual humor, which in many instances serves to relieve tensions in the work place. Cathy Young clearly states that there are serious cases of sexual harassment and again she provides examples of both the *quid pro quo* and the hostile environment types that should be against the law. She concludes by calling for a clear, objective definition of sexual harassment.

Shifting next to the domestic violence theme, Canadian sociologist Reena Sommer credits the women's movement for bringing the issue of wife battering to the forefront. But, Sommer argues, "the lobby for the protection of women has been at the expense of protecting other family members." She criticizes data sources that describe rates of violence committed by men and women and explains the need for surveys based on random samples of the general population, as a basis for determining rates of domestic violence and distributions of perpetrators and victims.

As a case in point, Canadian Senator Anne Cools cites the 1985 National Family Violence survey in which husbands were found to be the only violent partner in 25.9% of the cases, wives in 25.5% of the cases, and both husbands and wives were violent in 48.6% of the cases. Cools also cites the Ontario study of child abuse and neglect that found mothers were the perpetrators of 49% of the 46,683 cases of child abuse, neglect, or emotional maltreatment.

From the vantage point of a professor and practitioner of medicine, David Gremillion describes the biases he has observed in professional programs, among social science academics, and in the media against men, and for women. He quotes discussions in medical literature about the "suppression of the underclass by the surrogate patriarchy of medicine" and urges physicians and other professionals to make their goal the reduction of abusive and violent behavior by all family members.

House Congressional Staff member Carol Statuto Bevan answers the question she poses about how children fare under current welfare programs by showing that the welfare system's belief that children always do better by remaining or being reunited with their biological families, often works against a child's best interests. Bevan reviews studies that document that adoptive parents fulfill children's developmental needs, that the home environment provided by adoptive parents is conducive to child rearing, and that adopted children fare well.

Staff Attorney with the Institute for Justice, Donna Matias provides both a case study and a brief history of the obstacles families face who have tried to adopt across racial lines. Matias shows that even in states in which recent statutes bar race as a factor in adoption, social workers and adoption agencies place effective barriers against transracial adoptions, which result in minority children remaining in foster care and institutions longer than white children.

Father's rights advocate Ron Henry warns that "children are harmed when the unintended consequence of welfare policy is to favor non-working single parent households over all others." Attorney Henry proposes amendments to the welfare law that would eliminate the encouragement of intergenerational welfare dependency and that would promote the placement of children in non-welfare environments. "Family preservation," Henry insists, must be understood to include and encourage the participation of fathers.

In her chapter on custody and child support, Attorney Anne Mitchell provides interesting and surprising data on how mothers and fathers fare legally and financially after divorce. For example, in 1991, 24% of custodial mothers received no support compared to 37% of custodial fathers. In September 1995, U.S. Census data revealed that while 27.5% of noncustodial mothers have no time share privileges, 42% of noncustodial fathers have no time share privileges. This type of information is rarely found in the media, where the stories usually focus on deadbeat dads and the maternal bond.

In the section on the Use and Importance of Data, Professor James Lynch of the Department of Justice, Law and Society at American University explains why there can be widely different statistical estimates about the number of rapes and sexual assaults that are reported across studies. He explains how this variability has generated a great deal of controversy about the frequency of rape. Advocates of legislation that seek to reduce and redress violence against women have cited the higher figures while opponents of these bills have used lower estimates. The result has been not only a vitriolic and largely ideological debate over the issue and the bills, but also the trashing of social statistics customarily used to inform these discussions. The studies and statistical series have been portrayed as ideologically driven and are, therefore, dismissed. Lynch believes that this tendency to "deconstruct" social statistics from both ends of the ideological spectrum is dangerous. It undermines public confidence in statistical data, consigning policy debates to anecdote and ideology. This is not to deny that there are substantial difficulties in the measurement of rape. But, Lynch argues, these problems are knowable and can, perhaps, be fixed or otherwise taken into account. He concludes that, at minimum, having these debates about social statistics take place in the arena of scientific methodologies holds greater promise for understanding than arguments between advocates of substantive positions.

Continuing on the same theme, I describe examples about how data have been ignored, misinterpreted, denied or made up to suit political objectives on such issues as transracial adoption, immigration, the relationship between exposure to pornography and violent crime, and the explanations for why women engage in certain types of criminal activities.

The case of the missing report or "non-existent study" publicized by the American Association of University Women, asserts that teachers in elementary and middle schools give more attention and more esteem building encouragement to boys, prompted psychologist Professor Judith Kleinfeld at the University of Alaska in Fairbanks to conduct a classroom study on whether information can induce changes in attitudes about gender issues. Somewhat to her surprise, Professor Kleinfeld found that despite the political fervor that gender issues often evoke, students enrolled in an introductory psychology class were responsive to evidence.

In "Heterophobia: The Feminist Turn Against Men," Professor Daphne Patai of the University of Massachusetts at Amherst and co-author of *Professing Feminism*, a critical analysis of Women's Studies Programs, turns her analytical eye on the rhetoric of women who, in her view, have a "pathological aversion to men." She cites their rhetoric as being a language of hate. Patai believes that many of the leading spokespersons for the radical feminists have turned against men and that their views will have a strong negative influence on feminism in the future. The writings of these heterophobes, in Patai's view, have contributed to the creation of a climate in which individual autonomy is under attack.

Finally, Laurie Morrow, a Professor of English at Louisiana State University takes us on a nostalgic journey going back almost sixty years to 1939 when Clare Booth Luce's play *The Women*, appeared on the silver screen. To this day, never has a movie been made in which more women were more consistently portrayed as petty, destructive, mean spirited, and just plain bitchy. Laurie informs us that in a few months, shooting will begin on a remake of this classic but clearly politically incorrect film. I shall leave it to you to see how Laurie Morrow moves from her discussion of *The Women*, to the current feminist movement, to what Women's Freedom Network is all about. I think you will find it an interesting trip. She aptly describes Women's Freedom Network supporters as women who enjoy "a good laugh and a lively argument," who do not see themselves as victims and who share a commitment "that truth is best sought through reasoned discourse."

As this volume goes to press, plans for the Third National Women's Freedom

Network Conference are well underway.

*Rita J. Simon, President, WFN and University
Professor, School of Public Affairs and Washington
College of Law, American University, Washington, D.C.*

Affirmative Action: Creating a Crisis in a Free Society

Sally C. Pipes, President
Pacific Research Institute for Public Policy

Political scientist Harvey C. Mansfield Jr. once described affirmative action as "settling down in our constitutional polity like a determined guest seeking to establish squatters' rights." As you know, we have begun eviction proceedings in California. First, in June of this year, Governor Wilson signed an Executive Order ending race- and gender-based preferences in state hiring and contracting. Second, in July, the University of California's governing board voted to end racial preferences in admissions, hiring, and contracting. Third, and most fundamentally, a constitutional ballot initiative called the California Civil Rights Initiative, or the CCRI, could end all race- and gender-based decision making in California's public sector. Polls indicate the CCRI would pass by a wide majority if placed before the voters. The issue now is whether its sponsors can raise enough money to qualify the initiative for the ballot, which takes about $1 million in California.

Although the initial rumblings are coming from California, the rethinking of race-based preferential policies will not be confined to the Golden State. The coincidence of the CCRI's likely appearance on the 1996 ballot and President Clinton's bid for re-election has focused national attention on the initiative's fate. With 54 electoral votes, 20 percent of those needed to become president, California is a crucial state for any presidential hopeful. With all the attention focused on the CCRI, no candidate can avoid taking a position.

Early field polls find strong support for the initiative, with very few voters undecided.[1] Support is strongest among men at 61 percent but a majority of women polled, 52 percent, also favor the initiative.[2] Even in the liberal Bay Area, a poll of 600 adults conducted by the *San Francisco Chronicle* and KRON-TV found that 50 percent of those polled would support an initiative to end affirmative action as we have come to know it. Of the women polled, only 28 percent felt that women and minorities should receive preference while 36 percent felt that affirmative action meant fewer opportunities for white men. A quarter of the women polled believed that the push for equality has gone too far.[3]

Both sides of the initiative debate are paying close attention to the attitudes and concerns of women. As a majority of the electorate, the women's vote will decide the future of affirmative action. Broadening of opportunities has certainly helped many women advance in society, particularly in their careers. Since the late 1960s, the number of women in the labor force has increased dramatically in both the private and public sectors; women now hold 53 percent of all professional positions.[4] As women, however, we must sort out two things. First, is our success owed to quotas, as the so-called feminist leaders would have us believe, or to the changes in attitudes that opened the doors of opportunity? Second, most women are married to men with whom many have children, close to half of them male. In our multiple roles as professionals, wives and mothers, we must ask ourselves if the benefits we may receive from a continuation of outcomes-based affirmative action programs outweigh the harm, both financial and psychological, that these same programs inflict upon our husbands and sons. As care givers as well as breadwinners, women see both edges of affirmative action's sword.

This tension was apparent at a recent meeting of female business owners convened by California Governor Pete Wilson. While at least one woman vocally supported California's set-asides for women-owned businesses, from which she benefited, others were more circumspect. One woman who owned a business which contracted with the state unequivocally denounced the programs. Although she stood to benefit from them, she was insulted that the government felt she needed its protection. She also resented the fact that her son had been passed up for admission at the top University of California schools because, she believed, of race-based admissions.

Proponents of race- and gender-based preference policies know that if they are to defeat the CCRI they must convince women that we require affirmative action as it has come to be known. Women can expect a well-funded, highly sophisticated public relations campaign to try to convince us that without governmentally-induced preferential treatment, we will quickly find ourselves barefoot and back in the kitchen. In other words, the so-called feminist leaders and bureaucrats who purport to defend women from our "sexist society" need to convince women that without the government's protection we will be relegated back to the dark alleys of victimhood. After all, if we do not see ourselves as victims, then we will not depend on the services of those who would deliver us from victimhood.

The 1995 report of the President's Glass Ceiling Commission is the prototype for the propaganda soon to be hurled at women. As such, it merits addressing.

The report, issued in March of 1995, illustrates the panicked nature of the fight to maintain the federal government's affirmative action machine. The rhetorical underpinning of the *Glass Ceiling Report* is entitlement. Looking at the highest echelons of the country's largest companies and using outdated statistics, the study finds women and minorities noticeably absent, and based on this outcome-oriented approach, goes on to spend 200-plus pages concocting a blueprint for bureaucratically driven change. Its underlying demand is a guarantee that women hold a fixed percentage, a quota, if you will, of top executive positions.

The other hot button issue to mobilize women in support of special preferences is the gender wage gap. Fifty-nine-cent buttons have given way to 72-cent buttons, but the gist of the argument is very much the same: again, women are the victims of a sexist society.

These slogans are politically catchy but factually bankrupt. Since the mid-1970s, the gender gap in wages has narrowed at a rate compatible with the changes in market skills women have acquired. The slow rate of change decried by radical feminists is a mathematical artifact, a result of their propensity to compare apples to oranges in order to draw a conclusion about fruit.

When we compare apples to apples, this becomes clear. Differences in earnings are meaningless if the numbers are not corrected for years in the workforce, educational level, field of degree and marital status. When we dissect the data this way, we find good news for women, if not for proponents of affirmative action. As June O'Neill, director of the Congressional Budget Office, told us last year, for childless men and women who are 27-33, women earn 98 percent of the man's salary.[5] Similarly, the earnings difference among men and women who hold Ph.D.s in economics is a narrow 5 percent.

According to a recent study by Dunn and Bradstreet, there are currently 7.7 million women-owned businesses in the United States generating $1.4 trillion in sales.[6] These firms, with more than 15 million individuals on their payrolls, employ 35 percent more people than Fortune 500 companies do worldwide. Outside of the Fortune 1000, women hold 45 percent of all managerial positions.[7]

Women are clearly performing well in the marketplace. In terms of affirmative action, women must decide whether they need equality of opportunity or, as the radical feminists contend, they require heavy-handed government intervention. The data indicate that doing away with bureaucratic intervention will not affect women's chances for professional success.

After all, tomorrow's leaders are today's college students and today's college students are increasingly female. In the 1980s women received over half of all bachelor's degrees in the United States. The profile for top executives in a Fortune 500 company includes an MBA, but in 1971, women accounted for just under four percent of total MBAs conferred. That proportion jumped to over 34 percent by 1991[8]. In other high-wage fields, women have made similar strides. From 1970 to 1990, women jumped from just over five percent of law degrees awarded to more than 42 percent. And, over the same period, women moved from earning just over eight percent of medical degrees to earning over 34 percent in 1990[9].

Women are not the helpless victims that proponents of affirmative action so desperately want us to believe. Once the door cracked open, the floodgates burst. All indicators point to even greater achievement for women in every sector of society through the coming years.

Women must decide if the marginal benefits of bureaucratically enforced outcomes-based affirmative action are worth the additional costs. For women, a major cost of affirmative action is the stigma of being an affirmative action hire, something with which I am intimately familiar. Invariably, when I debate so-called feminists they assert that I have no right to criticize affirmative action because I owe my very job to it. While this is categorically untrue (something to which anyone who knows the composition of the board that hired me can attest), I am, nevertheless, assumed indebted simply because of the program's existence. This stigma, that women would not be at the top without the benevolence of enlightened liberal men and our feminist saviors, is unavoidable. It is also something that the next generation of women might be just as happy to do without.

A middle-aged nurse and educator from the Midwest made this point, posting on an America Online Bulletin Board, "Intelligent, hard-working blacks -- male and female -- who had earned respect and position are also resentful of the stigma that is attached to being the 'token black,' just as many women are tired of being the 'token female.'"

Mariana Parks, who is currently Vice President at the Seattle-based Washington Institute for Policy Studies, adds an interesting thought for women. Over the course of her career, which includes work in the private sector and in politics, on both sides of the aisle, she noticed that a mentor is extremely important for anyone who is serious about a career. "You learn your best lessons from the mistakes you make," says Parks, "but someone must be willing to sit down with you and tell you that you've screwed up. Now we have created a situation, with the deadly cocktail of affirmative action, EEOC lawsuits, and sexual harassment lawsuits, in which people are increasingly unwilling to tell women what they are doing or have done wrong because it creates a paper trail. In the long run, this will be a huge impediment to women's advancement."

If Not Affirmative Action, Then What?

Opponents of equality of results-based affirmative action must constantly answer the question: If not affirmative action, then what? The short answer is that discrimination is illegal and acts of discrimination should be dealt with on an individual level. The inherent injustice of current affirmative action programs, as University of Texas Law Professor Lino Graglia told the California Assembly Judiciary Committee in May, 1995, is that you cannot make up for discrimination inflicted upon A by B by discriminating against C in favor of D. Every act of discrimination has two parties and should be treated accordingly.

The longer answer however is philosophical. The fundamental problem of equality of results-based affirmative action is that it assumes free individuals left to their own devices will not manage their lives in a way that promotes the general welfare. As a result, partisans of equality of result-based affirmative action believe we need so-called enlightened social planners, which often turn out to be these very same people, to create a more just and equitable society. Advocates of freedom believe that individuals, while self-interested, are basically good and, given the right incentives, will make wise and prudent decisions. Advocates of bureaucratic control, in contrast, believe that humans are destructively self-interested and that without constant oversight and prodding from government officials, society would be chaotic and evil.

I shall conclude with the thoughts of Dr. Thomas Sowell, an intellectual giant, who has written profusely and eloquently about equality for many years. In his book *Conflict of Visions*, Dr. Sowell notes that classical liberals and those considered liberal by American standards[10] cannot even agree on what equality of opportunity means. For classical liberals, "as long as the process itself treats everyone the same -- judges them by the same criteria, whether in employment or in the classroom -- then there is equality of opportunity or equality before the law."[11] For American liberals, however, "equality of opportunity means equalized probabilities of achieving given results, whether in education, employment, or the courtroom."[12] According to Dr. Sowell's analysis, the original seed of affirmative action was poisoned by a fundamental disagreement over conceptions of equality. When free market individuals spoke of equality of opportunity, liberals heard equality of results.

Articulating a vision of a fair and just society is critical to resolving the debate over affirmative action. Dr. Sowell is again a beacon of light. He points out that classical liberals and American liberals view the abilities of the masses much differently. Classical liberals, knowing that knowledge is diffuse and discrete, view common people as more intelligent than do American liberals, who put their faith in expert knowledge. This leads to radically different policy prescriptions for the role of elites in society. Classical liberals believe "it is discretion which is to be equally and individually exercised as much as possible, under the influence of traditions and values derived from the widely shared experience of the many, rather than the special articulation of the few."[13] For American liberals, "it is the material conditions of life which are to be equalized under the influence or power of those with the intellectual and moral standing to make the well-being of others their special concern."[14]

The current debate over affirmative action provides an opportunity for advocates of freedom to follow the lead of such noted scholars as Thomas Sowell, and advocate true equality, which can only be equality of process if society is to avoid finite splintering of warring ethnicities and genders. Women play a central role in the dissemination of this message, because, in our multiple roles as daughters, mothers, sisters, wives and co-workers, we have the most to gain from freedom and the most to lose from the further balkanization in America.

End Notes

1. May 1995 Field Poll of 744 registered California voters showed 56 percent support. *San Francisco Chronicle*, June 6, 1995.
2. May 1995 Field Poll.
3. *San Francisco Chronicle*/KRON-TV Poll which was conducted April 27-30, 1995. Reported in *San Francisco Chronicle*, May 10, 1995.
4. *Op. Cit.*
5. June O'Neill. "The Causes and Significance of the Declining Gender Gap in Pay." Presented at the Women's Freedom Network Conference, October 2, 1994.
6. The National Foundation for Women Business Owners and Dunn & Bradstreet Information Services, April, 1995.
7. Ellen Ladowsky, "That's No White Male . . ." *The Wall Street Journal*, March 27, 1995, Editorial page.
8. U.S. National Center for Education Statistics, *Digest of Education Statistics*, annual.
9. *Ibid.*

10. Sowell does not use these categories in *A Conflict of Visions*. Instead, he uses "constrained" and "unconstrained" views of human nature to explain theoretical differences. This in-depth, penetrating, and eloquent analysis exposes the philosophical root of many political disputes. Though it deserves much more attention than we can herein afford it, I have chosen to use more familiar categories for brevity's sake.

11. Thomas Sowell, *A Conflict of Visions*, William and Morrow Company, 1987, p. 123.

12. *Ibid*.

13. *Ibid*, p. 140.

14. *Ibid*, p. 140.

Affirmative Action: An Economic Analysis

Deborah Walker, Associate Professor of Economics
Loyola University, New Orleans, Louisiana

Introduction

For the first time in over thirty years it is becoming socially acceptable to not only question the usefulness of affirmative action, but to openly oppose it. This may be due to the Supreme Court ruling in June of last year, which holds that Congress must meet an extremely stringent legal standard to justify any contracting or hiring practice based on race.[1] Furthermore, California, a leader in many political waves, is considering a constitutional amendment which would prohibit the state from granting preferential treatment to anyone in the public sector on the basis of race, sex, color, ethnicity, or national origin.

But on the other hand, perhaps this new opposition to affirmative action stems from the reality that affirmative action does not work; and the man and woman on the street have known this longer than has our government. Could it be that government is bending to a grassroots movement in this country which opposes preferential treatment on the basis of skin color or sex? If so, why does this grassroots movement exist? Why would anyone oppose affirmative action?

Before we address this question, let's first review the reasons affirmative action was applauded by many, and is still applauded by some. Its birth is usually attributed to the passage of the Civil Rights Act of 1964. However, many people feel this does an injustice to this Act, as well as to other Civil Rights decisions, such as the 1954 *Brown v. Board of Education* decision. This is because the meaning or ideal behind Civil Rights in the 1950s and 1960s was equality of opportunity, meaning that individuals should be judged on their merits *as individuals*. It was preferential treatment that these laws were designed to destroy. Affirmative action, on the other hand, "requires that they [individuals] be judged *with regard* to group membership, receiving preferential or compensatory treatment in some cases to achieve a more proportional 'representation' in various institutions and occupations."[2]

Some may not agree with this interpretation or definition of affirmative action, stating, for example that ". . . Affirmative action is about inclusion, not about quotas. It's about giving qualified women and minorities -- who have long been shut out -- a genuine shot at performing."[3]

Regardless, however, if one simply views Title VII of the Civil Rights Act as a means of attempting to achieve equality of opportunity and not as the beginning of special privileges, the very idea that discrimination based on sex should be prohibited is economically unsound and actually detrimental to women.[4] This is especially true when affirmative action legislation is defined by court decisions requiring specific results in markets. It would be hard-pressed to deny that, until recently, the courts *have* interpreted affirmative action as "preferential treatment" designed to achieve some desired quantitative result.[5]

This "results" oriented approach to affirmative action continues to be a popular basis for its support. *Good For Business: Making Full Use of the Nation's Human Capital*, published earlier this year and written by the Federal Glass Ceiling Commission headed by Labor Secretary Robert Reich, assumes repeatedly that if the percentage of women in a particular job does not equal the percentage of women in the labor force -- there is clearly a problem. As Reich writes, "In short, the fact-finding report (*Good For Business*) tells us that the world at the top of the corporate hierarchy does not yet look anything like America."[6] The presumption being, of course, that it *should*.

This presumption, or the "results principle" used by Secretary Reich, as well as by the Courts, makes the meaning of affirmative action to the average person clear: individuals should be subjected to different rules and standards if that means that a certain result will supposedly be attained.

As economist Thomas Sowell is perhaps best at pointing out, this "results principle" is based upon some important assumptions regarding discrimination. Sometimes these assumptions are stated, but usually as facts, not as assumptions. For example, *Good For Business* states that a report done in 1992 "revealed that *prejudice against minorities and white women continues to be the single most important barrier to their advancement into the executive ranks.*"[7] "Prejudice" meaning unfair discrimination, which causes poor representation of women and minorities (as compared to white men) in executive positions. What assumptions underlie this statement? Thomas Sowell explains:

> Several unspoken assumptions underlie the principle that statistical disparities imply discrimination. The first, and apparently most obvious, is that discrimination leads to adverse effects on the observable achievements of those who are discriminated against. The second assumption is that the converse of this is equally true -- that statistical differences signal, imply and/or measure discrimination. This assumption depends upon a third unspoken premise -- that large statistical differences between groups do not usually arise and persist without discrimination.[8]

There is no reason to believe, in other words, that there would be equal representation of women and men in all occupations *even in the absence of discrimination*. The fact is we do not know how many women would be in the top ranks of corporate America if we did live in a world where hiring was completely neutral with respect to sex. To say that the absence of women, or a small percentage of women in a particular occupation or rank, is mostly due to discrimination is to jump to a conclusion not supported by any concrete evidence or "proof." Statistical evidence does not prove nor disprove discrimination.

The purpose of this paper, therefore, is to demonstrate how and why affirmative action legislation designed to give special treatment to women, or simply designed to keep employers from ever considering sex as an employment criterion, is both economically unsound and detrimental to women. In so doing, freedom of contract will be provided as an alternative to affirmative action in addressing "sexism" in our society.

Sexism, Statistical Discrimination, and Subjective Perceptions

Before going further in the analysis, it is necessary to clarify the categories or meanings of what might be termed "sex discrimination."[9] This is especially important because the argument will be made later that some forms of sex discrimination are actually necessary or even desirable in free markets. The categories of sex discrimination include:

1. *Pure Sexism.* The offering of different contract terms (including no contract at all) to women based solely on group membership, not based on any other criteria usually used otherwise (such as skill, physical strength, education, experience, reliability, etc.). In other words, sexism exists whenever there is no *economic* justification for offering different contract terms to women relative to men. In this case an employer may even perceive a woman to be more qualified than a man but still refuse to hire her.

2. *Institutional Sexism.* The offering of different contract terms (including no contract at all) to an individual woman subjectively perceived as being less economically qualified as a man solely because she is a woman. The perception is not based on objective facts, but is based on presumptions about behavior. The presumptions may or may not have any basis in reality.

3. *Statistical Sexism.* The offering of different contract terms (including none at all) to women based on statistical averages of the relevant criteria for a job (for example, the average number of years women stay in a job relative to men, or the average number of times women take a leave of absence relative to men). It should be noted here that the statistical averages arise because of actual or objective differences between the behavior of men and women on the job.

4. *Economical Sexism.* The offering of different contract terms (including none at all) to women, judged as individuals, because no women meet the relevant criteria for a particular job. In this case the relevant criteria may include physical strength, or it may include the risk associated with the health or safety of a particular job (present or future). Examples here might include professional football or boxing, or a position which, because of chemicals used on the job, might harm the reproductive capability of a woman but not that of a

man. It should be noted that these examples may be irrelevant in the future because of changes in technology.

It is important to understand why an employer might choose to hire a man over a woman because, as stated earlier, the *reasons* behind the employment decision might be justified on economic, as well as moral, grounds. It is the first category, pure sexism, that most women, and indeed many men, find both unfair and downright repulsive. There are many who would also like to see both institutional sexism, as well as statistical sexism, either disappear or diminish.[10] The question, therefore, is what is the best means to achieving these goals? Is affirmative action the answer? Or is it part of the problem? Are there other means we should be exploring? The remainder of this paper addresses these questions.

Why -- And Why Not -- Affirmative Action

The reasons given in favor of affirmative action (defined as special privileges for women) are varied. They include: to prevent sex discrimination; to compensate for past injustices, which presumes a "social disadvantage" for women; and to promote the ideal of equality. Let's look at each one of these reasons with a critical eye.

To Prevent Sex Discrimination. There are three reasons why affirmative action should not be used to prevent sex discrimination: (1) Some sex discrimination is necessary and desirable, (2) there are better ways of decreasing or eliminating sexism in markets, and (3) affirmative action actually increases sexism.

(1) Desirable Discrimination

First, as stated earlier, some sex discrimination is necessary and desirable. In some cases discrimination will persist because it can be profitable. Most obvious is the fact that when employers decide to hire someone, they face a knowledge problem regarding which employees to hire. They must trade off the costs of screening individual employees with the costs of missing out on hiring very productive workers. Although firms, indeed market forces, have produced several ways by which employers can screen employees at lower costs, in many cases these costs remain high and employers resort to statistical sexism simply because it is profitable to do so. However, markets and individual women can decrease statistical sexism over time. This will be examined in a later section.

As another example of profitable sexism, consider a case where current employees, not the employer, prefer working with men rather than women. The employer may find it profitable to accept these preferences simply because it will decrease costs within the firm. When employees are diverse, the "governing costs" of reaching a consensus regarding rules within the firm can be very high. On the other hand, when employees are similar, they are more likely to easily and efficiently agree to rules, both formal and informal, that govern the work environment. In some cases, women may prefer to work with other women because, for instance, being more sympathetic to short-term periods of absence because of child care responsibilities, they are more likely to "cover" for their fellow female employees. A firm must therefore weigh these governing costs against the potential benefits of having a more diverse workplace. For example, if a firm's customers are primarily women, the firm may want to hire women who have special knowledge regarding how their products should be designed and marketed.[11]

To minimize conflict, groups may have a tendency to self-select. When the process of self-selection is unhindered, worker satisfaction will increase and, as Richard Epstein argues, the income of all workers may also increase. If, for instance, male chauvinists tend to group together in particular firms, then the rest of the workforce will not have to deal with them. As a consequence, although job openings in a particular firm may be reduced for any particular group of women, all other job opportunities for women will increase. Because the chauvinists are drawn to each other, women will find less discrimination against them in all other firms in the labor market.[12]

The bottom line is that firms should be allowed to discriminate if it is profitable for them to do so. This may be, at first glance, detrimental to women. But that is not true because the best economic environment for women -- whatever their lifestyle choices -- is one in which free markets are operating as efficiently (profitably) as possible. This is because it is this environment that creates the kind of opportunities women (and their husbands and children) need in order to live the kind of life they so desire.

Regulating a free economy decreases the efficiency of the economy. Jobs are created when resources are put to productive or more productive uses. This can only come about if resources, including human resources, are moved in directions that entrepreneurs freely choose. Entrepreneurs have their pocketbooks on the line and are closest to the problems at hand. They do not always make the right decision, but even their failures provide vital information to future entrepreneurs, and certainly no government agency can do a better job. Affirmative action legislation hinders the entrepreneurial process. Resources are used less productively, and new jobs are not created. Unfortunately, no one can point to a specific unemployed person and say he or she is out of a job because of affirmative action legislation. But any good economist can explain the relation of cause and effect.

(2) Decreasing Sexism

A second reason why affirmative action should not be used to prevent sex discrimination is that there are better ways of preventing, or at the least diminishing, undesirable sexism in markets. Discrimination against women in labor markets will decrease when it is in an entrepreneur's best interest. Discrimination on the basis of sex can be costly. Consider the case of pure sexism. If a firm decides that it will only hire men, for example, the firm must spend more time searching for qualified applicants who must also be men. The added search for men can be very costly, especially if there are very few qualified people in the relevant labor market. The discriminating firm can then face additional costs. In order to attract the few qualified persons to the firm who are men, it must pay them relatively higher wages. If other firms do not discriminate on the basis of sex, their labor pools are larger. They will not have to offer such high wages in order to attract qualified persons to their firms. Consequently, the discriminating employer faces higher costs in two ways: through longer and more extensive searches, the costs of which also include lost productivity, and through effectively decreasing the available (i.e., acceptable) labor supply, driving up the wages that the employer must pay.

Since firms only survive in markets if they make monetary profits, discriminating firms with higher costs will be at a competitive disadvantage and will either have to stop the discriminating behavior to remain competitive, or lose profitability and perhaps even close their doors. In this way, competition in markets can, at times, decrease pure sexism. However, the less competitive a market is, the more likely a discriminating employer will be able to bear the costs of sexism. For instance, in industries where there are legal restrictions to entry or in government-operated firms and nonprofit organizations, sexism is more likely to persist. Nonprofit or government-operated firms are not subject to competitive forces in the sense that they do not have to make a profit to survive. In essence, in many cases they can afford to discriminate when firms faced with more productive competitors cannot.

As hinted at earlier, in some cases third parties can be the real source of employer sexism. For example, customers or existing employees can insist that certain categories of potential employees be eliminated from consideration. As mentioned, because of this it can be sometimes economically desirable to discriminate. However, the market in some instances can also diminish third party discrimination. Customer discrimination, for example, can be reduced if customers do not have direct contact with all employees. Customers cannot push their preferences on an entire firm without assuming considerable costs. When one buys a loaf of bread, one does not usually ask the cashier if a woman or man baked it.

Turn now to the case of institutional sexism. In this case, when the employer is hiring based on subjective perceptions of the characteristics of an entire sex, whether the characteristics are real or falsely perceived is important. If the perception regarding the sex is incorrect, competitive forces will tend to punish discriminating employers. However, if employers are using statistical sexism and their information about the group is correct, women who fall in the upper range of the scale, i.e., those who are more productive than the average woman, will be punished because of their sex. Employers may decide to discriminate because the costs of screening individual women to discover if they fall in the upper range of the distribution will outweigh the estimated benefits of finding them.

On the other hand, most employers would rather screen individual employees and hire the most productive in any group. As mentioned earlier, they must trade off the cost of screening individual employees against the cost of missing out on hiring very productive workers. This is why markets have come up with different ways to screen employees at lower costs. Employers use employment agencies, interviews, references, a variety of tests such as aptitude or skill level tests, and they look for brand names in the educational and vocational institutions which potential employees attended. All these devices decrease screening costs for employers and thereby increase the likelihood that potential employees will be hired on the basis of their individual attributes rather than on the basis of their group membership.

Anything which increases the flow of information about individual employees will lead to a decrease in employer discrimination based upon group membership. To the extent that the flow of information is interrupted, employers' screening costs remain high and they resort to hiring on the basis of statistical averages. As a consequence, legislation that prohibits the use of employment tests or prohibits the asking of particular questions in employment interviews will actually decrease the likelihood that individual women can set themselves apart from the group and be hired on the basis of individual merit.

Of course, it should also be noted that this knowledge problem that employers face can be a source of opportunity for female employers. As women, they will sometimes have more knowledge about the true characteristics of individual women and will therefore be at an information advantage over other employers.

The employment contract itself is an important source of information for employers who are willing to hire from any group of employees, as long as they can in some way determine individual merit prior to employment. This is especially important for women, because it is through this means that statistical sexism can be decreased over time. Through individual contract terms a woman can assure an employer that she will not leave the job within a specific period of time, will not ask for an extended leave if she does choose to have a child, and so on. In other words, she can legally promise the employer that she will take full responsibility for her personal choices and will not expect the employer's costs to increase because of those choices. In this way, women who have chosen to make their market careers their top priority can signal that fact to employers and be judged on their individual merits. The freedom to make creative, individualized employment contracts can be a very important source of information to employers, and it can thereby decrease discrimination.

There are other ways discrimination can be overcome in free markets. When wages are free to vary as the market sees fit, discriminatory practices can be broken down. If an employer is faced with hiring a highly skilled male employee or a less-skilled female employee, an employer can be induced to hire the less-skilled woman if the difference in the wage rates between the two workers justifies the difference in productivity. Two important points must follow. First, if the perception regarding the skill or productivity level is correct, then hiring the less-skilled woman enables her to gain valuable experience and skills, increasing her market value and wage rate over time. Second, if the perception of productivity is incorrect, hiring a woman over an equally productive male at a relatively lower wage rate allows the woman to obtain the job and prove her productivity, thereby also allowing her to increase her wage over time -- sometimes almost immediately upon discovery that the employer's perception was incorrect.

Although the arguments I have summarized demonstrate how competitive markets can decrease discrimination, there are several reasons why discrimination will persist in many cases. First, markets are not static and the information contained within them is dispersed and constantly changing. As mentioned, while most employers attempt to hire the most productive employees, their inability to obtain information on individual applicants may cause them to continue using statistical averages.

Furthermore, because markets are dynamic and information is never perfect, markets are never perfectly competitive and monetary profits are never fully maximized. In fact, it is impossible for a firm to know if its profits are maximized. In reality, employers try to make enough monetary profit to satisfy the owners of the firm, so that the firm's resources will not be moved elsewhere. It may be the case that some employers are able to trade off monetary profit for personal satisfaction. In other words, because markets are not perfect, some discrimination may persist because employers would rather discriminate than make more money.

As I have mentioned, government barriers to entry, protective tariffs, minimum wage laws, and the like are also important reasons why discrimination remains in markets. These policies make markets less competitive, thereby allowing discriminatory behavior to persist.

(3) *Affirmative Action Increases Sexism*

And finally, the last reason affirmative action should not be used to decrease sexism is because affirmative action legislation, like all other labor legislation and/or mandates, actually increases the very thing it is designed to decrease. Sexism increases when legislation, including not only affirmative action but other labor market mandates (such as child care or family leave policies), increases the costs of hiring women over men. True, there are individual women who have jobs they would not otherwise have because of these mandates. But that does not mean discrimination has decreased or that we are better off as a society. On the contrary, many people are out of a job or are underemployed because of affirmative action and other labor mandates.

Furthermore, affirmative action legislation reinforces the idea that women are not truly capable of competing with men on an equal playing field. This is both insulting and detrimental to women. Special privileges can decrease the incentives of women to gain the skill, education, knowledge of the "corporate culture," or whatever else it might take to compete with men *under the same rules men face*.

Special privileges can have several negative effects. First, they actually give a grain of truth to the idea that women aren't as productive as men. If women do not have to be as productive as men to be rewarded in markets, many will not be. Those who do not let the special privileges diminish their incentives to better themselves are hurt by those women who do, because *all* women are perceived as less productive. Second, when men are faced with having to work harder than women in order to achieve the same status, resentment against all women increases. This resentment can take many forms, but one of them is an increase in pure sexism. And third, even when women do achieve success on the job, they often do not get the credit they deserve because the success is attributed to special privilege and not to hard work.

Compensation. Affirmative action is supposedly designed to compensate women for what was wrongfully done to them in the past. Certainly most would agree that history has seen its injustices toward women. It has been a relatively short period of time that women have been viewed as the moral equal of men. Because of this, women's rights to own property and to enter into contracts were nonexistent or limited. There were also many labor regulations which limited both the number of hours a woman could work and the variety of jobs she could apply for. It has only been 76 years since the passage of the Nineteenth Amendment -- affirming women as full citizens of the United States. And the list goes on. Clearly, women were disadvantaged in markets.

Can and should we compensate them for this past injustice? One major problem with attempting to do so by special privilege legislation is that this attempt aggregates all women into one category -- the repressed sex. The individual is lost. There may have been, or are, individual women who, from their point of view, benefitted from some of these past policies. Furthermore, there were, and are, probably many men who were hurt by them. The male child of a single mother unable to get employment comes to mind. Women's disadvantages due to past injustices cannot be changed or remedied by disadvantaging another group, because not all individuals within the group fit the "group profile." Instead, we should be trying to destroy disadvantages or barriers to individuals, regardless of group membership.

Along these same lines, another problem with the compensation idea is that in most cases those who did the injustice and those who suffered from it are not the same people subject to affirmative action. Is it right for a generation to pay for the injustices of the previous generation by giving special privileges to individuals who have never suffered an injustice? What affirmative action tends to do, therefore, is to promote intergenerational antagonism.

To Promote the Ideal of Equality. It is certainly a noble goal to promote "equality." But there are several definitions of "equality," and the promotion of one form can destroy the existence of another.

Equality of opportunity, for example, can mean that everyone should be able to offer their services for a given job. This means that if a woman wants to apply for a job, there are no legal restrictions keeping her from making an offer and there are no legal restrictions on the content of the offer, or on the acceptances of the offer (apart from force and fraud).[13] This is the definition of "equality" or equality of opportunity that best contributes to the well-being of women. This is akin to saying that men and women are equal in the eyes of the law.

However, equality of opportunity can have a different meaning. It can mean that employers have an obligation to consider everyone who makes an offer. Furthermore, certain characteristics of persons (such as sex, race or age) making the offers generally cannot be used as criteria by employers for choosing whether or not to accept the offers. This was the original intent of Title VII. Under affirmative action, however, equality has come to mean that the employer does have an obligation to consider everyone making the offers and can use sex, for example, as a criterion for employment, not in order to increase efficiency, but in order to achieve some *equal end result.*

Not only is this end-results approach a mistake because of its erroneous assumptions mentioned earlier, but also because it is impossible to achieve. Markets are complex and dynamic. Because of this, they cannot be planned with any degree of success. Attempting to plan out the market such that a specific number of women will hold certain positions, for example, will be futile. But just as important, this attempt will produce unintended and undesirable consequences, only some of which can be foreseen.

As explained earlier, it appears that some of the unintended consequences of affirmative action are an increase in sexism, a decrease in productivity, and an increase in bureaucracy. These certainly do not seem to be desirable social goals.

Markets and Opportunities

Freedom of contract, which is an underlying principle of markets, is the alternative women should turn to instead of affirmative action. One is hard-pressed to deny today that capitalist economies "work better" than do planned economies. What this means is that free markets lead the way to economic prosperity and growth, and a strong and prosperous economy is the only environment in which women can broaden their roles in the ways they desire. An opportunity is something that is seen as something desirable by an individual woman. Opportunities cannot be planned or mandated through affirmative action legislation.

There are many ways in which a strong economy creates opportunities. First and foremost is through job creation. Job opportunities, which are important because they allow women options in choosing an employer, are created by efficient markets -- markets where resources (including human resources) are allocated on the basis of productivity and *not on the basis of sex.* Efficiency creates opportunities. Efficiency is enhanced in environments where it is rewarded -- in free markets. When women call for special privileges which decrease the efficiency of firms, they are not only hurting their employers; they could be hurting themselves, or another woman (or man -- perhaps a husband or son) looking for a job.

Businesses have developed and should continue to develop creative ways to keep female employees happy and efficient. But these decisions must be left to individual firms and not mandated by government.

There are two other important ways economic freedom opens opportunities for women. First, markets created the technology which changed our economy from one based on physical strength (giving men a comparative advantage in many economic activities) to one where physical strength is not a prerequisite for economic success. And second, only a free market economy provides women the option of entrepreneurship. Women are now becoming market leaders in small business entrepreneurship. Women-owned businesses remain one of the fastest-growing segments of our economy and women continue to start businesses at twice the rate of men. U.S. Census Bureau statistics indicate that women will likely own 40% of the small businesses in the United States by the year 2000. Obviously, women entrepreneurs are a strong and growing economic force in the United States economy and warrant more attention from the business and academic communities than has previously been given.

Economic theory can tell us some things about why women are turning to entrepreneurship in such large numbers. First, new venture creation may be an opportunity for those women who have worked their way up the corporate ladder and feel that they have reached the so-called "glass ceiling." As much as markets have a tendency to decrease discrimination over time, some sex discrimination still persists for reasons mentioned earlier in this paper. Becoming one's own boss through entrepreneurship can be a way of skirting market discrimination.

Furthermore, it can also be an opportunity for those women who need a flexible work schedule and/or need to work out of their homes due to child care responsibilities. Entrepreneurship, especially on a small scale, can sometimes allow women greater flexibility than working for someone else would allow. In other words, often times women face different circumstances than men do because of family responsibilities.

Second, because women themselves are often the most frequent customers in the very service industries in which they tend to start businesses, some women may have unique knowledge about a particular service that men, in general, do not have. This knowledge can then give women a competitive advantage in starting and running a successful business. The key is that these women are becoming alert to this knowledge. This demonstrates how women can, when they take responsibility for their own lives, create their own opportunities.

Affirmative action, instead of being the friend to women it was promised to be, has not only *not* helped women, but has actually worsened their position in society. Women should instead rely on individual responsibility and free markets to achieve the respect and equality under the law they so rightly deserve.

End Notes

1. *Adarand Constructors, Inc. v. Pena*, 115 S.Ct. 2097(1995).

2. Sowell, Thomas. 1984, *Civil Rights: Rhetoric or Reality?* New York: William Morrow, p. 38.

3. Price, Hugh B. "Affirmative Action: Quality Not Quotas," *Wall Street Journal*, August 18, 1995, p. A8.

4. Although there is the exemption to Title VII which states that men and women can be treated differently when sex is a "bona fide occupational qualification reasonably necessary to the normal operation" of a business, this exemption has not eliminated special treatment for women even when it might be economically detrimental.

5. As examples, in *United Steelworkers v. Weber*, 443 U.S. 193 (1979), the Supreme Court held that racial quotas are permissible under Title VII and in *Johnson v. Transportation Agency*, 480 U.S. 616 (1987), the Court held that it was not a violation of Title VII for the county of Santa Clara in California to promote a female employee over a more qualified male worker in order to remedy "underrepresentation" of females in certain job categories. The Civil Rights Act of 1991, however, seems to have shifted attention away from disparate impact cases to claims based on the standard theory of intentional discrimination. This is because the Act created new schemes authorizing compensatory and punitive damages in cases involving intentional discrimination.

6. *Good for Business: Making Full Use of the Nation's Human Capital*, March 1995, Washington, D.C., U. S. Department of Labor, p. iv.

7. *Ibid.*, p. 6.

8. Sowell, 1984, pp. 16-17.

9. These categories are somewhat similar to Thomas Sowell's categories regarding race discrimination as presented in *Markets and Minorities*, 1981, New York: Basic Books, Chapter Two.

10. And there are those who also think that economic sexism should also be abolished — that either the economic reasoning should be secondary to a higher moral argument, or that what we think are differences between men and women are only cultural constructs. If we change the culture, we will abolish these differences. This paper does not agree with this point of view.

11. Epstein, Richard A. 1992, *Forbidden Grounds: The Case Against Employment Discrimination Laws*, Cambridge, Massachusetts: Harvard University Press.

12. *Ibid.*, p. 68.

13. *Ibid.*

Affirmative Action: A View from the Barricades

Tama Starr, President
Artkraft Strauss Sign Corporation, New York

Sensitive, compassionate people -- like you and me -- appreciate the benevolent impulses underlying Affirmative Action. Less well-known is the cost, in terms of money, time and sheer brain damage, that putting this doctrine into practice actually entails. As the employer of 87 skilled workers in three construction trades, plus support staff -- who have always come in all colors, races and genders without any help whatsoever from me -- I've experienced first-hand the excruciating visceral reality of complying with affirmative action's sexist and racist bureaucratic jihad.

I submit for your disbelief an actual contract that my company undertook last summer. It is a typical contract that anyone in the construction trades would recognize. Accompany me on a journey through it. Your benevolence will never be the same again.

The job itself is straightforward, consisting of the fabrication and installation of a set of fifteen-foot-tall metal letters on the roof of a factory building. Doing the work is child's play compared with following the contract.

The distinguishing features of the project are: a) the "progressive" character of the customer, a large publisher; and b) my city government's corporate welfare policy which, by supporting the project with tax abatements and other incentives, subjects it to the same EEO requirements as a public project. Thus, there are four levels of affirmative action: corporate, city, state and federal.

The contract itself, printed in normal-size type, is only two and a half pages long. It says, in essence, "You do the work, and we will pay you." Then there is a Scope of Work, describing the work, and a set of drawings depicting the work. There is a set of "Special Conditions," perfectly normal, containing provisions for *force majeure*, change orders and warranties, and a discussion of the sales tax exemption. There is a standard form of insurance certificate.

And then there is a 101-page Exhibit comprised of twenty separate documents embodying the affirmative action requirements.

Let's have a look at some highlights.

The first document is the oxymoronically named "Affirmative Action/Non-Discrimination/MBE-WBE Requirement." It lists "participation goals" by trade: for example, Carpenters on this job are expected to be 42.74% Minority and 1.58% Female. Iron Workers, both Ornamental and Structural, are to be 58.53% Minority and 7.63% Female. There is no clue as to how these numbers were derived, but you can immediately see the value of a Minority Female Iron Worker. Don't think, however, if you are fortunate enough to have access to one, that you can circumvent the requirements by transferring her around, or by renting her to or from a competitor. The document sternly warns:

Compliance by [sic] the Contractor's specific affirmative action obligations required herein of minority and female employment and training must be substantially uniform throughout the length of this Trade Contract and in each trade. The transfer of minority or female employees or trainees from contractor to contractor or from project to project for the sole purpose of meeting the Subcontractor's goals shall be a violation of this Trade Contract.

We are a Union shop, which means that we hire only from within the unions' respective labor pools. On their part, the unions maintain quality control, putting all the workers through apprenticeship and education programs. But they never promised (who would have thought to ask?) to provide Painters who are 62.57% Minority and 3.52% Female, as required here. And, warns the document, "neither the provisions of any collective bargaining agreement, nor the failure by a union" to refer the correctly-composed work force "shall excuse the Contractor's obligations hereunder."

So we are commanded to direct our recruitment efforts "to schools with minority and female students, to minority, female and community organizations, and to minority and female recruitment and training organizations" and to keep careful records of the disposition of minority and female job applicants who come in off the street. But we can't hire off the street. No matter. We are not only required to "meet with union officials to inform them of the policy" and to "bargain with respect to the inclusion of [the policy] in all union agreements," but also to report any noncooperation by any union to the proper authorities, failure to report being itself a misdemeanor. This will certainly do wonders for our relationship with the unions (who, in fairness, are feeling the heavy hand of these requirements at least as keenly as we are).

Next, the document lists sixteen "specific affirmative actions" to be taken, the first of which is to "assign two or more women to each Phase of the construction project." Now here's a problem. One of my Phases is structural installation, which entails landing big steel and welding it while perched on a scaffold a hundred feet or more above the ground, sometimes in zero-degree weather. For some reason, I don't get a lot of female applicants for this position. So if you know of any women -- preferably minority and, even better, disabled -- who would enjoy this work, please send them over!

I suppose I could halfway comply with this provision by assigning myself. But in conjunction with the female-assignment provision is the statement that I will "ensure and maintain a working environment free of harassment, intimidation, and coercion." And with all this, I don't feel free of harassment, intimidation and coercion at all. But maybe I'm not supposed to: I'm the Boss, so I'm not in a Protected Class.

The rest of the sixteen points (two pages of very small print) describe, in exquisite detail, the special recruitment, monitoring, notification, review and record-keeping procedures to be undertaken with respect to hiring and cultivating minority and female employees. Most noteworthy here is the invasion of their privacy. I am required to "encourage present minority and female employees to recruit other minority persons and women." What form is this "encouragement" supposed to take? "Hello, Ms. Wong, I see you are Asian. Got any sisters at home?"

My favorite paragraph in this document is what I call the "desperate" clause. It reads as follows:

> (j): Goals for minorities and a separate single goal for women have been established. The Contractor, however, is required . . . to take affirmative action for all minority groups, both male and female, and all women, both minority and non-minority. Consequently the Contractor may be in violation hereof if a particular group is employed in a substantially desperate [sic] manner (for example, even though the Contractor has achieved its goals for women generally, the Contractor may be in violation hereof if a specific minority group of women is underutilized).

So even after I've desperately hired Ms. Wong's sister as a high-mast welder, I may still be in trouble if there aren't enough female Aleuts or Samoans on the team.

Part II of this document provides for "meaningful participation" by Minority Business Enterprises and Women-Owned Business Enterprises (MBE/WBE). What is "meaningful participation"? It is defined in italicized type:

> *"Meaningful participation" shall mean that at least seventeen percent (17%) of the total dollar value of the construction contracts (including subcontracts) covering the Work are for the participation of Minority Business Enterprises and Women-owned Business Enterprises, of which at least twelve percent (12%) are for the participation of Minority Business Enterprises and at least 5% [sic] are for the participation of Women-owned Business Enterprises.*

This section provides interesting ideas for the restructuring of one's business, including forming joint ventures or partnerships with MBEs and WBEs, and "not requiring bonds from and/or providing bonds and insurance for MBEs and WBEs," even, or especially, where one is required to provide bonds and/or insurance oneself. Again, there are impeccably detailed record-keeping requirements, including, most notably, "the reason for such decision" when any of the required discussions with MBEs and WBEs fail to result in a joint venture, partnership or subcontract.

Part III summarizes and incorporates by reference Mayoral Executive Order #50, which emphasizes, among other things, that the Contractor "will not discriminate. . . on the basis of . . . race, color, creed, national origin, sex, age, handicap, marital status, sexual orientation or affectional preference." (What, may

And does it matter, at least until the lawsuits come?) That is all very nice, but on the previous page, the Contractor was *required* to discriminate, that is, to intervene positively, on the basis of race, sex, etc. Oh, well.

This is not trivial. E.O. #50 provides for the Department of Labor Services to have access to all of your "books, records and accounts" to ascertain compliance. And the DLS can *hurt you bad* if you are not in compliance. They can not only void your contract, withhold payment for work you've already done and "reduce the Contract payments by a percentage equal to that designated as the business enterprise goal percentage," but also [50.65B(iv)] physically enter into your premises and "impose an employment program." But do not feel your rights are unprotected. The DLS can impose these sanctions only "after a hearing, held pursuant to the rules of the DLS."

The "employment program," by the way, may include sentencing your workers to "participation by minority, female and handicapped employees in career days, job fairs, youth motivation programs, and related activities in their communities." I'm sure they'll love that. But they've no choice. Among the crimes that can bring the wrath of the DLS down upon you is that your "Minorities, women, handicapped, or older employees are excluded from or *are not participating in* [italics mine] company-sponsored activities or programs." Your non-minorities, however, can apparently skip the company picnic with impunity.

The climax of the document is the Contractor's agreement "to include the provisions of the foregoing paragraphs in every subcontract or purchase order to which it becomes a party . . . so that the provisions will be binding upon each Contractor or vendor." An interesting infinite recursion. The "foregoing paragraphs" include their own inclusion -- so all subordinate contractors and vendors are required to include them in *their* subcontracts and purchase orders, ad infinitum. Clearly the intention is to infect the whole of the commercial community like a disease.

The dénouement is a promise to "refrain from entering into any contract . . . with a subcontractor who is not in compliance with the requirements of E.O. #50 and the rules and regulations promulgated thereunder." Now, how, exactly, is one supposed to know who is and who is not in compliance with the "requirements of E.O. #50," etc.? But any failure to comply with any part of the agreement is a "material breach," and subject to the punishments described above.

The second document is the customer's "EEO/Payroll Package," which, we are informed, has helpfully "been prepared to assist each Contractor/subcontractor in meeting all Equal Opportunity/Affirmative Action requirements for this project." Item I reiterates the 17% M/WBE goal and instructs the Contractor on the proper, appropriately complex procedure for submittals of "documented efforts" to meet the goal. Item II, "Minority and Female Workforce Participation Goals," requires compliance with "the Federal goals for the construction industry" (included later), and reiterates the "participation goals" of the various construction trades. It is interesting to note that while Operating Engineers are required to be 46.52% Minority and 9.26% Female, Cement Masons, required to be 37.73% Minority, are

Minority and 9.26% Female, Cement Masons, required to be 37.73% Minority, are required to be but 0.00% Female. Is this a misprint? Who is protecting the oppressed Female Cement Masons? Class action, anybody? Item III reiterates the requirement for compliance with E.O. #50, and also requires "attendance at all meetings requested by the monitoring agency, the Division of Labor Services." (Estimating Department: Did you put this into the price?)

Items IV-VII delineate the differences in reporting requirements between contracts over and under $1,000,000 and companies over and under 100 employees. When contracts and companies grow past a certain size, the reporting requirements increase exponentially. Even Forrest Gump (a Protected Person under the ADA) would recognize the importance of keeping all contracts under $1,000,000 and all companies under 100 employees. "Smaller is better" is now apparently public policy.

Items VII-XVII (there are two Items #VII) list and describe the forms, certificates, documents, reports, letters and statements required to document compliance. Item XVIII, "Sexual Harassment Fact Sheet," says, "Each Contractor must include this fact sheet in all subcontracts." Another virus: each subcontractor must include it in all of his subcontracts and purchase orders, and require those subcontractors and vendors to include it in theirs. It includes idealized examples of sexual harassment that not even your most imaginative subcontractors can have thought of. Won't it be fun when they disseminate it to their workforce!

The next document is Mayor's Executive Order #50 itself (29 pages of tiny, single-spaced type), so you can't claim you haven't read it.

Next is the city's required "Construction Employment Report" (7 pages), of which perhaps the most interesting part is a chart delineating "for each trade currently employed by your company . . . the current workforce. . ." include: Males (1) White (Non-Hisp.), (2) Black (Non-Hisp.), (3) Hisp., (4) Asian, (5) Native-Amer.; and (6)-(10), Females, same categories. These charts must be filled out for (J) Journey level workers, (A) Apprentices, (H) Helpers, and (TRN) Trainees. In our case, we must fill out these charts twelve times, to cover all four levels of workers in each of our three trades -- and submit them monthly. The submitting Contractor must also attach to these reports "All Collective Bargaining Agreements, Employment Application [sic], EEO Policy Statement and your most recent EEO-1 Report." Somebody up there sure loves paper!

What puzzles me is why these charts are restricted to race and sex: why don't they include religion, age, marital status, sexual orientation, affectional preference, etc.? How else can I prove my innocence? But I'm sure we'll get around to that. The precedents are there.

Next are the actual "Less Than One Hundred (100) Employees Certificate" and the "Less Than $1,000,000 Subcontract Certificate," each bearing a legend to the effect that any incorrect data "may result in criminal prosecution."

Next is the "Boilerplate for Equal Employment Opportunity Statement," a resounding personal affirmation by the company's CEO (me!) stating that "We will take specific action to ensure that applicants are employed and that employees are treated during employment, without regard to their race, creed, color, national origin, sex, age, disability, marital status, sexual orientation or citizenship status" (clearly a lie, given the rest of the documents) and announcing that "(Name) has been appointed Director of our equal employment opportunity programs and will report directly to me on the results of such program [sic]." Interesting here is the implied admission of guilt. "(Name) responsibilities [sic] include . . . assisting in the identification of problem areas" and "assisting line management in arriving at solutions to problems." The possibility that there are no problems does not exist.

A small but far-reaching statement: "To ensure adherence to this policy, performance evaluations for supervisory personnel shall include ratings on their equal employment opportunity efforts and results." Some companies actually take this seriously. "Sorry, Sally. Your team invented a better mousetrap and added fifteen million dollars to our bottom line. But they were the wrong color, so it doesn't count."

"Additionally," the "Boilerplate" goes on to say,

> . . . in furtherance of our equal employment opportunity commitment (Contractor name) shall *insist* [italics mine] that labor unions and other recruiting sources actively recruit and refer members of all protected groups for all positions, incorporate non-discriminatory provisions in all its contracts and purchase orders [more virus again] and include the EEO logo, slogan or statement in all solicitations or advertisements for employees.

How, I wonder, is my "insistence" to be measured? Is it worth a dollar an hour for all employees? Ten dollars an hour? Because in labor negotiations, every "insistence" has a price.

The next document is the "Contractor's Affirmative Action Plan," containing a chart called "Summary of Bid Activity with MBE and WBE Subcontractors/Vendors" that requires a listing of "all unsuccessful M/WBE subcontractors/vendors" by Name, Trade/Item, Date and Amount of Bid Submitted, Date of Elimination, and Reason for Elimination. Below, above the Notary seal, is a space for "Additional explanation of elimination: Include meetings held for negotiation, etc. (Use additional sheet if necessary)." I can easily imagine that any of the ordinary reasons for turning down a vendor or sub -- bad reputation, inability to perform work, criminality -- might be considered to have a racist component and thereby seal one's doom.

Then comes the "Contractor/Subcontractor Affirmative Action Commitment," requiring the Contractor to swear fealty once again by initialing various affirmations; and the weekly "Wage Requirement Letter," including space for each worker's name, address, social security number, race, sex, work classification, hours worked, rate of pay, deductions and net wages. Interesting, again, how much privacy the workers give up for the privilege of participation in this Brave New Nondiscriminatory World. The document also contains a separately-signed affirmation that "Contractor/Subcontractor certifies compliance with all Federal, State and Local EEO Requirements" (as if one could possibly understand what they are), and a statement that "The wilful [sic] falsification of any of the above statements may subject the Contractor or subcontractor to civil or criminal prosecution see section 1001 [sic] of Title 18 and Section 231 of Title 31 of the United States Code." This part is in *teeny-tiny* print and very difficult to read.

The next five pages, apparently handwritten by a diligent sixth-grader, are instructions on How to Complete the Payroll Forms. It has many helpful hints. Under "work classification," for example, it instructs, "Fill in the classification exactly as it appears on the determination. If classification is for a power equipment operator, indicate type, size, horsepower." But it does not ask for the color of the horse.

The next document, "Workforce Projection," is important because it offers a rescue for those contractors whose race and sex composition is below par. It allows you to anticipate compliance by listing, for each job category (Brick Masons, Equipment Operators, etc.) your "Current Employees to be Assigned to Contract," both "None-Minority [sic]," M and F, and "Minority," M and F, and the "Projected New Hires" within these categories that will bring you into compliance. It ends,

> The Contractor acknowledges that, to the extent that this workforce projection does not reflect anticipated achievement of the goals for minority and female employment contained in the contract for work on this project, it will work closely with the general Contractor and resourse [sic] and referral sources to identify, consider, and employ qualified individuals whose participation will enable the contractor to achieve the goals.

Now, that's a break!

Next is Form OC-257, the "Monthly Employment Utilization Report," which lists, for all trades and classifications, by "Work Hours of Employment (Federal & Non-Federal)," the "Total All Employees By Trade (M,F); Black (Not of Hispanic Origin) (M,F); Hispanic (M,F); Asian or Pacific Islander (M,F); American Indian or Alaskan Native (M,F);" and Total Percentages broken down by Minority, Female, Minority and Female vs. Total Number of Employees, and Total Number of Minority Employees broken down by Male vs. Female. You won't have failed to notice -- especially if you are the person filling out the forms -- that these race classifications are different from the ones required above. This Report must be submitted monthly, and needless to say, any inaccuracy in this chart constitutes a crime.

For those whose skills at statistical analysis may be sub-par, help is available. See Mayor's Executive Order #50:

> *50.51(D)*: The statistical criteria for evaluating the composition of the Contractor's workforce will be the following:

(i) the term "underutilization" means a statistically significant disparity between the employment of members of a racial, ethnic, or sexual group and their availability as determined by the Bureau utilization analysis; and (ii) the term "utilization analysis" will mean an analysis of the Contractor's workforce using standard statistical techniques to test a null hypothesis that utilization of a given protected group is within acceptable limits, given its availability. For the purpose of these regulations, the null hypothesis will be rejected (i.e., underutilization will be assumed) whenever there is reason to believe that the utilization rate is below the availability rate at the 80% level of significance.

Got it? Good.

The next documents are: a Sample Letter requesting Apprentice Certificates for personnel meeting the approved race/gender tests; a helpful list of "Recruitment Sources for Minority/Female Construction Workers"; and the "Sexual Harassment Fact Sheet," an interesting document that goes to considerable lengths to expand the definition of sexual harassment beyond the ordinary "most widely recognized pattern . . . in which a male supervisor sexually harasses a female employee."

The last document in the package is 26 pages in two columns of tiny print: Part 60-3 of the Office of Federal Contract Compliance Programs, the federal "Uniform Guidelines on Employee Selection Procedures." There are discrepancies between it and E.O. #50 and the other documents, but what do you do? You are a contractor with a workforce to support, and you want the job. So you close your eyes and hope for the best.

I had to send my new Director of EEO Compliance (formerly the payroll manager) to school in New Jersey for two days to learn how to fill out the reports for this contract. The presumption of racial and sexual villainy criminalizes everybody and creates a world of litigation. The paperwork required to comply with the contract nearly outweighs the steel. It also makes us the laughingstock of the world.

I discussed this phenomenon with the Dallas-based CEO of another company in my industry that is four times the size of mine. He said, "Sure, good companies run away! You won't see me bidding on any kind of government or government-subsidized work." So the government will get what it wants: contractors whose race/gender composition meets government goals, while taxpayers, as usual, foot the bill: in increased costs, in substandard work, and in the payroll of the genetically approved bureaucrats who scrutinize the reports.

But let's not despair. If we accept these conditions as facts of life, we have the opportunity for a happy solution. The problem, especially for smaller companies without millions of employees, is that while the goals are exact, the means of meeting them are crude. How do you really know that your Electricians are 33.99% Minority and 1.84% Female, as required? The loss of one worker of the approved hue may necessitate the termination of another of an opposing hue, to maintain the desired balance. This is unfair. But genetic analysis can solve all that.

Hardly any Americans today are racially "pure." Up to 95% of those checking many of the categories on the census form could just as well check "multiracial" if that were an option. Over the past 203 years since the first U.S. census, we have used at least 26 racial categories because we couldn't decide what they are; currently, such groups as Arab-Americans and Azorians (Afro-Portuguese) are lobbying for their own classification. Advances in biotechnology should enable us to end the confusion. We can investigate the DNA of all job applicants and candidates for promotion, isolate racial markers, and, by means of simple, weight-averaged mathematics (per E.O. #50), identify the individual workers whose characteristics we require.

From there, it is only one small step to the genetic engineering that will enable us to *create* the sociobiologically desirable workforce of the future. Want a Female Operating Engineer who is one-third Caucasian, one-twelfth Pacific Islander, one-quarter Hispanic, one-sixth Asian and one-sixth African-American? No problem! This will require some 20-year advance projections, but isn't that economic planning at its best? I can foresee platoons of forepersons, journeyfolk and apprentices, all genetically predisposed to their assigned occupations and trades, and all of the exact racial, ethnic and even hormonal mix that Nondiscrimination requires. What a beautiful, inspirational, politically-correct, glorious Rainbow it will be!

I can hardly wait. Can you?

Sexual Harassment: Is There A Better Way?

Cathy Young, Columnist, *Detroit Daily News*
and Vice President, Women's Freedom Network

It has been four years since Anita Hill accused Supreme Court nominee Clarence Thomas of sexually harassing her, an episode which certainly redefined the sexual harassment issue in this society. In a way, however, it only brought to the surface conflicts and paradoxes that had existed in the legal and social arena for some time. Starting around 1987, business magazines were warning managers about the pitfalls of new harassment laws which defined "hostile environment" so loosely and subjectively that no one could know when they might be crossing the line.[1] This flurry of articles stemmed from the Supreme Court's unanimous ruling in *Meritor v. Vinson* (1986), which established the principle that sexual conduct sufficiently "severe and pervasive" to create "an abusive working environment" should be treated as a form of sex-based discrimination.

There are several problems with this law. One is the sex discrimination model. When the first sexual harassment lawsuits were filed under civil rights laws in the 1970s, the courts generally rejected this line of reasoning, pointing out that, first, the sexual harassment of an employee by a co-worker or supervisor was not company policy (unlike, for instance, not hiring women for certain jobs or paying them less) but the behavior of an individual acting on his own, and also that such behavior was generally directed not at women as a class but at one particular woman -- and could, moreover, be directed either at a man or at a woman or both. Later rulings rejected these arguments, but they have never been effectively refuted. Even feminist legal scholar Susan Estrich recognizes that to "fit such cases into the Title VII rubric by pretending that they are no different than wage cases or other working condition cases" is "a disaster in doctrinal terms," making the issue of sexual coercion "legally invisible."[2]

Take, for instance, the issue of same-sex harassment. Many courts have ruled that a man who is subjected to unwelcome sexual overtures by a gay supervisor is indeed sexually harassed in the legal sense. Recently, however, the complaint of a male public utility employee in Baltimore who claimed that his boss had sexually harassed him by asking questions about his sex life, pointing a magnifying glass at his crotch, and making sexually suggestive comments was rejected, partly on the grounds that the supervisor was alleged to have behaved just as badly toward female employees. The U.S. District judge who dismissed the case indicated that he did not believe federal legislation was meant to cover same-sex sexual harassment. The Fourth U.S. Circuit Court of Appeals upheld the dismissal of the case but split over the basic issue of whether Title VII covers same-sex harassment.[3] In another case, a shy, sexually inexperienced man was tormented by male co-workers in ways that would amount to a clear case of harassment if directed at a woman -- lewd taunts, obscene pictures shoved in his face, being poked in the buttocks with a stick

-- and was found to have no legal case, since his tormentors' behavior was obviously not based on anti-male prejudice.[4] The Supreme Court has refused to tackle the issue; in 1993, it let stand a lower court ruling that complaints of harassment involving two heterosexuals of the same sex were not actionable.[5]

And there is the theoretical dilemma of the bisexual boss who makes sexual advances to both sexes. Or suppose that a male supervisor harasses women while a female or gay supervisor at the same office harasses men, effectively equalizing working conditions for both sexes. Would all of that be exempt from sexual harassment law?

In the arena of sexual discrimination law, sexual harassment is probably unique in that it does not require showing any damage to the victim. The latest Supreme Court ruling in *Harris v. Forklift* establishes that even psychological damage is not required. The only thing that needs to be shown is that the conduct is sufficiently severe to create a hostile environment for a reasonable person, and that it treats people differentially on the basis of gender (which could obviously include requests for dates). At the same time, many sexual harassment decisions seem to require that men and women be treated differently: profanity and sexual references that would be acceptable in an all-male environment are labeled sexual harassment when directed at women. This paradox was unwittingly summed up by actor and talk show host Charles Grodin when, on a program devoted to sexual harassment, he offered this advice on how to avoid improper behavior: "Treat a woman exactly like a man: 'Hi, How are you,' that's it. If you want to share sexual jokes with your co-worker, don't tell them to a woman. Otherwise, treat men and women exactly the same."[6]

Some court decisions have explicitly stated that sexual images, even if they seem to target men and women equally, are discriminatory to women. This was the case in the 1993 ruling of a federal district court in Florida in *Cardin v. Tropical Fruits, Inc.*[7] Barbara Cardin, an office worker dismissed as a part of staff reductions, sued alleging sex discrimination in pay and promotions as well as a "sexually hostile and offensive work environment." The court found no merit in the former claim but upheld the latter, finding that the company tolerated a "pervasive and continuing pattern" of sexual harassment that mostly involved raunchy cartoons and jokes. Most of the cartoons mentioned in the ruling seemed to make fun of *male* anatomy: an obese naked man viewing his genitals through a periscope, or a woman peeking under the sheets at her mate with the caption, "Where's the beef?" Cardin also claimed to have been offended by two rather juvenile written jokes circulating at the office and given to her by a *female* manager. Judge Stanley Marcus conceded that the cartoons and jokes "depicted both men and women" and that women participated in the bawdy humor. However, he wrote,

> widespread verbal and visual sexual humor -- particularly vulgar and degrading jokes and cartoons repeatedly disseminated in the workplace -- may tend to demean women. This is because such joking defines women as women by their sexuality, and consequently may create practical obstacles . . . in the workplace.[8]

Judge Marcus also ruled that office gossip about Cardin's supposed affair with a co-worker constituted gender-based harassment, since, even though the rumor obviously concerned the man as well, it "created an issue of Plaintiff's sexuality in the context of her work . . . identifying her not as a worker, but as a woman-worker."[9] This reasoning and this language come straight from the argument of radical feminist theorist Catharine MacKinnon, who wrote in her ground breaking 1979 book *Sexual Harassment of Working Women* that the definition of sexual harassment as sex discrimination rests on the theory that "sexuality largely defines women as women in this society, so violations of it are abuses of women as women."[10] Not coincidentally, MacKinnon is also known for such pronouncements as, "[H]eterosexuality . . . institutionalizes male sexual dominance and female sexual submission."[11]

During the Hill-Thomas controversy, many feminists assured the public that no one was trying to stamp out sexuality -- only abuse of power. Nevertheless, distinctions between unwelcome sexual conduct by people in authority and by co-workers (or fellow students) of equal status are increasingly being blurred. In a 1994 survey of federal workers, about 12 percent of the women reported experiencing unwanted sexual attention from someone in a position of authority over them. But the survey treated unwelcome sexual comments, jokes, and overtures from peers or even subordinates just as seriously, bringing up the overall proportion of women who were harassed to well over 40 percent.[12]

And many personal accounts of so-called "harassment" certainly seem to have less to do with power than with sexual interest. Writing in *The Progressive*, New York free-lance journalist L. A. Winokur describes such an episode: a man who was one of her regular sources told her over drinks that he had always wanted to have an affair with her. She made it clear she wasn't interested, and he left her alone. "Whether or not it constituted harassment may be up for grabs," the author adds grimly, "though I certainly know where I stand on the matter."[13] From this, one can obviously conclude that (1) women are extremely thin-skinned and (2) the expression of any sexual interest in a woman with whom one has some professional contact, even with no coercion involved, is improper. Ironically, Winokur then goes on to repeat the obligatory mantra: "Sexual harassment is not about sex; it's about the abuse of power."

The fact is that to some radical feminists, *all* sex is about power. MacKinnon's views are not unique. Feminist sociologists Barbara Gutek and Vera Dunwoody make a distinction between sexual harassment and "nonharassing" behaviors such as sexual compliments, jokes, or requests for dates by co-workers; but, in a curious choice of words, they label these behaviors as "sexual nonharassment" (which is akin to referring to consensual intercourse as "sexual nonassault" or "nonrape") and suggest that such interactions may be detrimental to women even if the women are not aware of any harm.[14] And Boston University law professor Kathryn Abrams writes: "Because of the inequality and coercion with which it is so frequently associated in the minds of women, the appearance of sexuality in an unexpected context or a setting of ostensible equality can be an anguishing experience." Abrams, whose works have been quoted in appellate court rulings on sexual harassment,[15] grudgingly acknowledges that "many women hold positive attitudes about uncoerced sex" but seeks to balance this assertion with a reference to Andrea Dworkin's *Intercourse*, as if positive female attitudes toward consensual sex and Dworkin's view -- summarized by Abrams as "sexual intercourse is inherently coercive and contributes inevitably to the subordination of women" -- were equally common.[16]

The assumption that "sexualization" in the workplace demeans women has trickled down into the culture as well as the courts. Consider Charles Grodin's admonition to treat a female co-worker exactly like a man (except for not telling her dirty jokes): this standard obviously presumes that there is not going to be any consensual flirting, not to mention sexual or romantic relationships, between male and female co-workers. The same message is conveyed by another piece of advice for the perplexed: "Don't do anything to a woman that you wouldn't do to Mom."[17] Sometimes, the guidelines get confusing: Helen Norton of the Legal Defense Fund suggests that a good test for harassment is "whether the defendant would have said the same things to his or her daughter, mother or wife. Or did the employee have to put up with something men did not have to put up with?"[18] -- as if there were no differences between the way a man talks to his mother, to his wife, and to other males.

All this raises the question: what do women really want in the workplace? It is a well-known fact that many people, perhaps most people today, meet their future partners either at work or through work-related contacts. Some advocates of stringent sexual harassment policies have pointed to surveys showing that most women would be offended if a co-worker directly propositioned them for sex. But does this in any way prove, as feminist legal theorist Susan Estrich has suggested, that most women are not interested in sexual or romantic relationships at work?[19] Surely, a direct proposition for sex is not a typical way to initiate a relationship.

To answer the question of what working women really want, one might honestly consider the question of whether women themselves behave in the workplace as if their sexuality were irrelevant. Are we to believe that women do not flirt, do not try to make themselves sexually attractive to men, do not judge men's sexual attractiveness, do not make sexual jokes? Indeed, popular women's magazines unabashedly offer tips on workplace flirting and office romances.[20] Are we to believe that women do not enjoy and participate in raunchy humor and sexual banter? Indeed, quite a few sexual harassment cases that have come before the courts suggest that they do. In one such case, a female flight attendant filed a sexual harassment suit against USAir claiming that a male pilot had sang lewd limericks to her and had once dropped on his knees and pretended to sniff at her crotch. Witnesses testified that on various occasions, the plaintiff, Betsy Swentek, had engaged in the following behaviors: she had put a dildo in her female supervisor's locker to "loosen her up"; she had handed a cup of her own urine as a "drink" to another employee; and she had grabbed a male pilot by a certain part of his anatomy with "a frank invitation to a sexual encounter."[21] All of which, of course, could have been construed as sexually harassing conduct, except that its targets did not complain -- maybe because they didn't think they were supposed to go to pieces just because a co-worker did something offensive.

Remarkably, the Fourth Circuit Court of Appeals found for Swentek, stating that the "[e]mployee's use of foul language with sexual innuendo in consensual setting did not waive her legal protection against unwelcome sexual harassment."[22] In other words, a woman can engage in lewd behavior at work and then complain when someone else engages in lewd behavior toward her. And then feminists make fun of men who are confused by the new standards!

Party-line feminists vigorously dispute the notion that the courts are clogged with trivial charges of sexual harassment. In fact, there are probably not too many preposterous cases that reach the courtroom -- though there are certainly a few. Take the case of former Wal-Mart salesclerk Pamela Kimzey, who was awarded $50 million in punitive damages in November 1995 (later reduced to $5 million by the presiding judge) due to alleged sexual harassment by her supervisors.

In July 1988, Kimzey went to work as a clerk in Wal-Mart's receiving department, where her supervisors included Henry Brewer and Mike Mais. She quit in January 1989 to care for her ailing mother. In April 1989, she went back to work and specifically asked to go back to the receiving department because she enjoyed the atmosphere. In February 1992, all receiving department employees except Brewer were reassigned to the night shift; about a month later, Kimzey asked Mais, by then the store manager, to put her back on the day shift and he granted her request. Shortly afterwards, she found that it was difficult for her to work with Brewer, who had recently lost his wife and, she believed, had started drinking heavily. He often yelled at her and once called her a "darn dummy" for using a scanner improperly. In February 1993, Kimzey complained to assistant manager Marci Turner, saying that Brewer was "jumping all over her." Turner conveyed her complaint to Mais, who talked to Kimzey and then to Brewer and reported the results of his investigation to the district manager. However, since he could not smell liquor on Brewer's breath as Kimzey had claimed, and could not confirm Brewer's intoxication, he believed he had no reason to punish him. In April, Kimzey decided to quit her job, even though Mais offered her other positions within the store in which she would not have had to work with Brewer.

Unpleasant though it may have been, Brewer's conduct did not seem to involve anything sexual. While Kimzey asserted that he treated women more harshly than men, her own witnesses contradicted her, saying that Brewer "yelled at about everyone that worked back there" and was equally nasty to men and to women. Where, then, did the sexual harassment come in? To make her case, Kimzey was allowed to testify about incidents that occurred during periods when she herself admitted she did not consider her working environment to be hostile or sexually abusive: a vulgar joke Brewer made at some point during her first stint at Wal-Mart in 1988-89 (when she was standing bent over with her back to him, he said something about finally knowing where to put a screwdriver), and the fact that, during the same period, Mais would allegedly playfully "kick" women in the legs. Never mind that Kimzey herself asked to return to that horribly hostile environment and indicated in her worker evaluation that she enjoyed the informal atmosphere at work.[23]

It may well be that the majority of cases that go through the legal system are far more substantive. But the real damage of sexual harassment hysteria occurs in what legal scholars call "the shadow of the law." The simple fact is that no employer wants to be sued, even if he or she eventually wins the case. And since employers can avoid liability by having a sexual harassment policy of which employees are aware, and by taking complaints seriously and handling them efficiently, they have an obvious incentive to err on the side of regulating behavior that might even remotely be considered actionable. In addition, sexual harassment consultants, lawyers, and corporate officials in charge of harassment policies obviously have an incentive to interpret offenses broadly, or at least not to discourage overreaction. (Many of the consultants also endorse the radical ideology that treats all "sexualization" of women as demeaning.) A typical 1995 article in *Industry Week* lists such forms of harassment as "suggestive remarks," "teasing and taunting of a sexual nature," "sexual bantering," "office or locker-room pinups," and "compliments with sexual overtones" (without even the "unwelcomeness" qualification) and warned, "Companies should not tolerate such behavior from their workers at any time."[24] This is also standard advice dispensed by lawyers and harassment consultants, whose trade is booming. One veteran consultant, Seattle-based human resources professional Chuck Hatten, who markets a "Sexual Harassment Prevention Board Game" as a training tool for corporate workshops, suggests that if a new employee joins an office where several workers have a habit of trading sexual jokes and is unhappy with these jokes, it is the employer's obligation to take whatever action is needed to put an end to such humor. Honeywell's 1990 harassment handbook lists "staring" as an offense; Boeing outlaws "blonde" jokes.[25]

At AT&T in 1992, Holt Euliss, a 36-year-old engineer with an impeccable work record, committed suicide after being subjected to draconian disciplinary measures because he told a mild off-color joke to a female clerk with whom he sometimes worked on the same floor at the company's North Carolina office, and touched either her upper torso (according to him) or her breast (according to her) in re-enacting the joke's pantomime about a tailor who tries to feel up a female client under the pretext of brushing a chalk outline off her dress. The woman, Angela Rhew, reported the incident to her boss, who told a sexual harassment officer to look into it. Euliss admitted the joke but denied the fondling. He was marched off the premises in front of all his co-workers and told to turn in his ID and not come back until further instructions.

Euliss' co-workers could not believe that this shy, mild-mannered man would grab a woman's breast. The case was further complicated by the relationship between Euliss and Rhew, who had known each other for years and were both recently divorced; he clearly took an interest in her and would do odd jobs around her house and coach her son for Little League. There is some indication that she was, perhaps, beginning to find his attention tiresome, though she apparently never said anything until that day.

Euliss' punishment was a thirty-day suspension without pay, a reduction in his benefits package, and almost literal exile to Siberia -- reassignment to a job involving on-site work on projects as far away as Alaska. A journalist who tackled the case received information suggesting that "AT&T needed a significant sexual harassment settlement" to show investigators from the Labor Department's Office of Federal Contract Compliance, who get suspicious if they see too few complaints being prosecuted.[26] Euliss' suicide came two days after he was informed of AT&T's decision; he was particularly distraught since the new job would take him away for months at a time from his daughter, of whom he shared custody with his ex-wife. AT&T later settled a wrongful-death lawsuit from the Euliss family, without admitting wrongdoing. This was the second time that an AT&T employee killed himself after being harshly disciplined on a minor charge of sexual harassment.

In a less dramatic case in 1992, Ron Contino, a senior vice president of the New York City Transit Authority, was demoted and smeared in the tabloids over a single inappropriate joke. At home recuperating from heart surgery, 56-year-old Contino was talking to a meeting of his staff by speakerphone and had an untimely attack of humor. Referring to "an old Arab custom" that "you have to prove yourself after a serious illness," he asked TA vice president Velva Edwards to rent a large auditorium "so you and me and Pat [Patricia O'Brien, general manager of Manhattan buses] can have sex on the stage."[27]

When the story got out, Contino was quick to apologize to his staff, and personally to O'Brien and Edwards. The "victims" were willing to put the incident behind them, and Edwards stressed that Contino had done a lot to help her career. But TA President Alan Kiepper was not mollified and punished Contino with a demotion and a pay cut for a remark "demeaning to women."[28]

As men learn to play the victim game, women too get caught up in the net. In 1994, several female tellers at United Jersey Bank decided to have some laughs with a co-worker and put two cutouts of male nudes from *Playgirl* on her counter; the woman laughed "hysterically," and two female managers joined in. (It was half an hour before closing time, and there were no customers in the bank.) A 25-year-old male teller decided to take offense and complained to the management. Five women were called on the carpet and told to apologize. They were suspended without pay for as long as two weeks, and some were demoted.[29]

What are the problems with the status quo? First of all, the current sexual harassment orthodoxy leads to a far-reaching effort to sanitize the workplace in ways that may make the work environment more "hostile" for some people (the use of sexual humor, for instance, may serve the legitimate purpose of relieving tension). It also promotes the disturbing idea that sexuality is demeaning to women; at the same time, it polarizes the sexes and sets up different standards for women and men, thus undermining the very ideal of equality it supposedly seeks to foster. Somehow, we are simultaneously promoting the idea that marriage is an equal partnership with shared responsibilities, *and* that men should not view their female peers in the workplace as potential sexual partners.

Moreover, this orthodoxy has established a dangerously subjective standard by which a major civil offense is defined. One EEOC official has defended the focus on the woman's response rather than the man's intent, saying by way of analogy, "If I run a stop sign, I have broken the law even if I did not intend to."[30] But the analogy is wrong. Even if you fail to see a stop sign, it remains a part of objective reality; it is hardly in the eye of the beholder. Traffic laws modeled on sexual harassment regulations would have no stop signs, traffic lights, or speed limits; you could be fined for failing to stop at an intersection when another motorist expected you to yield or for driving at a speed that made another driver or pedestrian uncomfortable.

The subjectivity of the law is underscored by a very clever study conducted recently by two University of Arizona psychologists. Two hundred and fifteen college women read a scenario of a male-female interaction, with a photo of the man below, and were asked to rate on a scale of 0 to 6 how sexually harassed they would feel in the woman's place. In the vignette, a student working as a part-time researcher at a prominent law firm is approached in the back of the firm's library by an employee who has unsuccessfully asked her out several times; he says he finds her very attractive and invites her for a drink after work. The man was variously described as either married or single and pictured as either attractive or unattractive. Did it make a difference? Absolutely. The mean "harassingness" rating was 2.68 for the single man and 3.28 for the married man; advances from the attractive suitor got a mean rating of 2.71, compared to 3.23 for his dorky-looking counterpart. Only two percent of the women who read the script featuring the handsome bachelor indicated that they would feel very harassed (a rating of 6), compared to 11 percent when the man was good-looking but married, 14 percent when he was single but plain, and 24 percent when he had the misfortune of being neither single nor sexy.[31] Extending the traffic-laws parallel, this is rather like letting a shiny new Volvo go faster and turn at more intersections than a battered Toyota.

Finally, the orthodoxy encourages people not to solve problems on their own but to run for help to Daddy -- or Mommy. Yes, if talking to the offender doesn't work, there should be another recourse. But official intervention should be the last, not the first resort.

Where do we go from here? Serious cases of sexual harassment, in which someone is forced to work in truly intolerable conditions, do exist. There is broad consensus, even among the severest critics of the harassment hysteria, that *quid pro quo* harassment -- the "sleep with me or you're fired" variety, or sexual blackmail -- should be against the law. There are also "hostile environment"-type cases where it is clear that the purpose of sexual conduct is not to engage in banter, to be funny, or to form a romantic bond, but to hurt and humiliate. In one particularly egregious case, three women hired to work as "flag persons" with an all-male road crew quit after a campaign of abuse in which crude propositions and obscene insults scrawled on a woman's dusty car were the mildest offenses. The men exposed themselves, urinated into a woman's water bottle, and grabbed at the women's breasts and thighs after trapping them between two trucks; once, a woman was forcibly lifted by a crew member and groped by others -- while a supervisor stood by and did nothing.[32]

Certain kinds of sexual advances with no *quid pro quo* element can also be so outrageous as to warrant legal actions. Some of the stories told by the women who came forward with charges against Sen. Bob Packwood -- being forcibly grabbed, fondled, and pushed against the wall -- would be in that category.

How, then, do we separate the wheat from the chaff? Do we just throw up our hands and say, "I know sexual harassment when I see it?"

Political scientist Ellen Frankel Paul, in an insightful 1990 law review article, proposes removing sexual harassment from the arena of federal civil rights law (eliminating the discrimination angle) and making it a state tort, similar to intentional infliction or emotional distress. Harassment would be defined as "sexual propositions incorporating overt or implicit threats of reprisal, and/or other sexual overtures or conduct so persistent and offensive that a reasonable person . . . would find it extreme and outrageous." Liability would require intentional or reckless acts by the harasser and "economic detriment and/or extreme emotional distress" to the victim. (The employer would be liable if he was notified of the harassment and took no action, or failed to provide an adequate complaint mechanism.)[33]

Another possibility is to limit "hostile environment" sexual harassment to acts that would fall under some type of criminal statute, at least a misdemeanor (from sexual assault to lewd and indecent behavior), and hold employers liable if they knowingly permit such activity to go on in the workplace. Some people may object that this would remove all verbal harassment, even of the most extreme kind, from the scope of legal action. If verbal harassment is to be proscribed, however, it would not be too much to at least stipulate that a "hostile environment" should require some actual hostility. This could be accomplished by amending the current Equal Employment Opportunity Commission formula -- conduct that has "the purpose or effect of unreasonably interfering with an individual's work performance or creating an intimidating, hostile, or offensive working environment" -- to read "purpose *and* effect." In the truly egregious cases such as that of the "flag girls," the plaintiffs should have little difficulty proving malicious intent or, at the very least, recklessness -- i.e., that the defendant acted in ways that any reasonable person could be expected to understand were abusive.

A clear and objective definition of sexual harassment would not only ease the present tensions between the sexes. In the long run, it would also help in the effort to curtail sexually abusive behavior at work and in schools, by eliminating the present resentment against the harassment crusade and preventing the issue from being trivialized into irrelevance.

End Notes

1. See, e.g., Marisa Manley, "Dealing With Sexual Harassment," *Inc.*, May 1987, p. 145; Walter Kiechel, "The High Cost of Sexual Harassment," *Fortune*, September 14, 1987, p. 147; Michael A. Verespej, "'Hostile Environment': It Has Made Sexual Harassment a Mine Field," *Industry Week*, March 21, 1988, p. 21; Gretchen Morgenson, "Watch That Leer, Stifle That Joke," *Forbes*, May 15, 1989, p. 69.

2. Susan Estrich, "Sex at Work," *Stanford Law Review*, 1991, v. 43, pp. 813-861 (at p. 820).

3. See Mark Guidera, "Court Dismisses BGE Same-Sex Harassment Case," *Baltimore Sun*, March 7, 1996, p. 1C; Kim Clark, "Man-to-Man Harassment in the Spotlight Today," *Baltimore Sun*, September 28, 1995, p. 1C; Kim Clark, "Same-Sex Harassment Suit Against BGE Dismissed," *Baltimore Sun*, December 30, 1994, p. 1A.

4. *Goluszek v. Smith*, 697 F. Supp. (N.D. Ill. 1988). More recently, the complaint of a male public utility employee in Baltimore who claimed that his boss had sexually harassed him by asking questions about his sex life, pointing a magnifying glass at his crotch, and making sexually suggestive comments was rejected partly on the grounds that the supervisor was alleged to have behaved just as badly toward female employees (Mark Guidera, "Court Dismisses BGE Same-Sex Harassment Case," *Baltimore Sun*, March 7, 1996, p. 1C; Kim Clark, "Man-to-Man Harassment in the Spotlight Today," *Baltimore Sun*, September 28, 1995, p. 1C; Kim Clark, "Same-Sex Harassment Suit Against BGE Dismissed," *Baltimore Sun*, December 30, 1994, p. 1A). The U.S. District judge dismissed the case indicating that he did not believe federal legislation was meant to cover same-sex sexual harassment. The 4th U.S. Circuit Court of Appeals upheld the dismissal of the case but split over the basic issue of whether Title VII covers same-sex harassment.

5. UPI, "Court Rejects Heterosexual Harassment," October 11, 1993.

6. CNBC, *Charles Grodin*, May 30, 1996.

7. *Cardin v. VIA Tropical Fruits, Inc.*, 7 Fla. Law W. Fed. D456 (1993).

8. *Ibid.*, p. 46.

9. *Ibid.*, p. 45.

10. Catharine MacKinnon, *Sexual Harassment of Working Women*. New Haven, CT: Yale University Press, 1979, p. 174.

11. Catharine MacKinnon, *Toward a Feminist Theory of the State*. Cambridge, Mass.: Harvard University Press, 1989, p. 113.

12. "Responding to Harassment," *The Washington Post*, March 13, 1996, p. A19.

13. L. A. Winokur, "The Sexual-Harassment Debates," *Progressive*, November 1993, p. 37.

14. Barbara Gutek and Vera Dunwoody, "Understanding Sex in the Workplace," in *Women and Work: An Annual Review*, v. 2, 1987, pp. 255, 258.

15. See, e.g., *Robinson v. Jacksonville Shipyards* and *Ellison v. Brady*, 924 F.2d 872, 879 (9th Cir. 1991).

16. Abrams, K. "Gender Discrimination and the Transformation of Workplace Norms," *Vanderbilt Law Review*, 1989, v. 42, pp. 1183-1248, at 1205, 1209.

17. See, e.g., Christine Bertelson, "A Simple Test for Harassment," *St. Louis Post-Dispatch*, September 6, 1994, p. B1.

18. Quoted in Leah Beth Ward, "Zaring Suit Puts Gender-Based Remarks on Trial," *Cincinnati Enquirer*, February 26, 1995, p. E1.

19. Estrich, "Sex at Work," p. 860 (n. 72).

20. See, e.g., "How to Make an Impact on a Man," *Cosmopolitan*, February 1989, p. 177.

21. *Swentek v. USAir*, 830 F. 2d 552.

22. *Ibid.*

22. *Ibid.*

23. This account of *Kimzey v. Wal-Mart* is based on appellate briefs by the appellee and the appellant filed with the U.S. Court of Appeals for the Eighth Circuit (No. 95-4219, Cross-Appeal No. 95-4220).

24. Michael A. Verespej, "New-Age Sexual Harassment: An Increasing Number of Victims Are Men or Same-Gender Workers," *Industry Week*, May 15, 1995, p. 64.

25. See Joann S. Lublin, "Companies Try a Variety of Approaches to Halt Sexual Harassment on the Job," *Wall Street Journal*, October 11, 1991, p. B1; Elizabeth Rhodes, "The Work World's Next Frontier," *Seattle Times*, October 16, 1992, p. D1.

26. Christopher Byron, "The Joke That Killed," *Esquire*, January 1995, pp. 84-90. The account of the Holt Euliss case is derived primarily from the articles by Byron and Lewis, as well as interviews with Richard Warren, the attorney who represented the Euliss family in its lawsuit against AT&T, and Dr. David Gremillion, who testified as an expert witness for the plaintiff in pretrial depositions.

27. Ellis Henican, "No Laughing Matter at TA: 'Stupid' Joke by Bus Boss Proves as Funny as a Flat Tire," *Newsday*, January 30, 1992, p. 3.

28. Quoted in Nat Hentoff, "Sexual Harassment by Speaker Phone," *The Washington Post*, March 14, 1992, p. A23.

29. Alex Michelini, "Male Teller Can't Bear Nudie Pix," *Daily News*, January 16, 1995.

30. Charles Looney, director of the EEOC New England office, quoted in Nancy Gibbs, "Office Crimes," *Time*, p. 53.

31. Virgil L. Sheets and Sanford L. Braver, "Perceptions of Sexual Harassment: Effects of a Harasser's Attractiveness." Paper presented at the conference of the Western Psychological Association, Phoenix, AZ, 1993. Additional materials provided in a personal communication from Dr. Virgil Sheets (currently at Indiana State University). The photos were selected from a singles magazine and "pre-rated" for attractiveness by female graduate students.

32. *Hall v. Gus Construction Co., Inc.*, 842 F.2d 1010 (8th Cir. 1988).

33. Ellen Frankel Paul, "Sexual Harassment As Sex Discrimination: A Defective Paradigm," *Yale Law & Policy Review*, v. 8, No. 2, 1990, p. 362.

The Dangerous Drift of "Harassment"

Eugene Volokh, Professor
UCLA Law School

What do the following have in common?

1. An employer says to an employee, "sleep with me or I'll fire you."
2. A woman's coworkers regularly try to fondle her; though she protests to management, management does nothing about it.
3. A woman's coworkers often call her "slut" and "bitch"; a black man's co-workers call him "nigger."
4. A partisan of one candidate for a union post takes a picture of the candidate's opponent (a 62-year old woman), attaches it to a *Hustler* centerfold, and distributes it to some coworkers.
5. Workers regularly use job titles such as "foreman" and "draftsman."
6. An employer puts Bible verses on its paychecks and religious articles in the employee newsletter.
7. Penn State University hangs a reproduction of Goya's *Naked Maja* in a classroom.
8. A library employee hangs up a *New Yorker* cartoon, printed in the wake of Lorena Bobbitt's amputation of her husband's penis; the cartoon shows one fully dressed man saying to another, "What's the big deal? I lopped off my own damn penis years ago."
9. A graduate student at the University of Nebraska puts on his desk a 5"x 7" photograph of his wife in a bikini.
10. To illustrate the concept of intentional action, a seminary professor uses a Talmudic story in which a man falls from a roof onto a woman and they accidentally have sex.
11. A man asks an acquaintance out on a date. The acquaintance says "No."
12. A high school boy looks at a girl in a sexual way; the girl doesn't like it.

The answer is: According to some, each of them is harassment -- sexual harassment, racial harassment, or religious harassment. Numbers one through six are harassment according to the courts. Numbers seven through nine were harassment according to employees, who lodged harassment complaints with their employers -- in each case, the employer, quite probably conscious of the risk of a lawsuit, ordered the offending behavior to stop. Number ten was harassment according to the school at which the professor was teaching. Numbers eleven and twelve are harassment according to two academic studies, both of which got extensive media coverage.

Both the law and social convention have begun to more and more forcefully condemn "harassment." In many cases that is all to the good. But in recent years, "harassment" has gotten to be a dangerously broad and vague concept. It has begun to pose serious free speech problems, and to touch conduct that is at most juvenile or mildly rude, or sometimes even perfectly innocent. In doing this, it risks crushing many innocents under its wheels, and risks hurting genuine harassment victims by seriously cheapening the coin of the "harassment" allegation.

Harassment Law

Most workplace harassment cases litigated in the U.S. are brought under Title VII of the Civil Rights Act of 1964, the landmark antidiscrimination law. Title VII does not specifically prohibit discrimination; it bars discrimination based on race, sex, national origin, and religion in the "terms, conditions, or privileges of employment."[1] But through the 1970s and early 1980s, courts have concluded that the ban on discrimination also prohibits two other things:

- "Quid pro quo" harassment -- sexual extortion of the "sleep with me or I'll fire you" variety.
- "Hostile work environment" harassment -- speech or conduct that is sufficiently "severe or pervasive" to create a "hostile or abusive work environment" because of a worker's sex, race, religion, national origin, age, or disability.[2]

The ban on "quid pro quo" harassment seems to me to be eminently proper, and it is also generally relatively narrow and well-defined. But the "hostile work environment" standard -- "severe or pervasive [enough to create] a hostile or abusive work environment" -- has proven to be a different story.

Hostile work environment harassment potentially covers quite a broad area. It is not limited to physical abuse (which it quite properly punishes) or repeated unwanted sexual advances or slurs (which raise more problems, but which I think can be restricted). Any sort of speech or conduct that -- in the eyes of the jury -- creates a hostile environment based on race, sex, religion, and such can be actionable. Thus, courts have read it to cover:

- The Bible verses in the paycheck and Christian-themed articles in the newsletter (mentioned above), on the theory that they create a hostile environment for a non-Christian employee.[3]
- The picture of the union candidate superimposed on a centerfold.[4]
- A Seventh Day Adventist's religious proselytizing, which apparently did not use any religious slurs but simply condemned others' religions.[5]
- The use of sex-based job titles such as "foreman" and "draftsman."[6] [A Kentucky state agency has in fact gotten a company to change its "Men Working" signs (at a cost of over $35,000) on the theory that the signs "perpetuate a discriminatory work environment and could have been deemed unlawful."][7]
- An employee's hanging "pictures of the Ayatollah Khome[i]ni and a

burning American flag in her own cubicle."[8]

- "[C]aricatures of naked men and women, animals with human genitalia, . . . a cartoon entitled 'Highway Signs You Should Know' [which showed] twelve drawings of sexually graphic 'road signs' (... for example, 'merge,' 'open road,' etc.)." The cartoons and jokes, while sexually themed, were apparently not misogynistic or sexist.[9]

All this, it seems to me, is squarely protected by the First Amendment.[10] Offensive as some of this speech might be to some -- and the union candidate incident, for instance, strikes me as extremely offensive -- the Constitution protects offensive and bigoted speech as well as the fine and the exalted.[11]

But even setting aside the Constitution, it just seems fundamentally unhealthy for the legal system to concern itself with minor slights such as the "foreman" incident or the sexual cartoons or the Bible verses. Is the greater goal of justice or equality or even civility served by a legal system that turns minor rudeness and insensitivity into grounds for a lawsuit?

The Wages of Vagueness

Harassment law, moreover, restricts more than just what the courts have specifically described as "harassment." Like all vague laws, it creates a twilight zone of ambiguous conduct, conduct which is neither clearly forbidden nor clearly permitted, and which cautious people are therefore wise to avoid.

Imagine that you are an employer, and one of your workers alleges that another's speech was "harassing"; this could be a cartoon or a poster or a joke or a political discussion in the lunch-room. The worker demands that such speech be banned.

You ask your lawyer whether you have to give in to the complaintant's demands, and he says, "Who can tell? I don't know whether the conduct was 'severe or pervasive' enough to create a 'hostile or abusive' environment. No one knows, at least until a jury decides. But look at it this way: If you take no action, you might get sued, and you might lose. If you tell the offending employee to shut up, though, you'll protect yourself from liability."

This reasoning, it seems to me, is how we get incidents like the ones with Goya's *Naked Maja*, the *New Yorker* "penis" cartoon, and the graduate student's wife in a bikini. The risk of liability, combined with the law's vagueness, creates a huge incentive to overcensor. These incidents, by the way, are far from unique,[12] and are quite understandable: The law cannot ban "pornography" (as harassment law does, on the theory that it creates a hostile environment for women) without affecting "legitimate" art.

Of course, it is always hard to tell to what extent the employers here were really influenced by fear of liability. One can imagine an employer restricting its employees just to keep up morale and avoid workplace tension. But in the *Naked Maja* incident, the employer specifically cited the risk of liability as part of its justification.[13] And employment lawyers are certainly advising employers to tread very carefully indeed. One writes, for instance:

> Suggestive joking of any kind must not be tolerated ... At the very least, you must insist that supervisors never engage in sexual joking or innuendo [;t]hat also goes for employees who hope to be promoted into supervisory positions ... Nip these activities in the bud ... Don't let your employees [p]ost pin-up photographs on the walls, [or t]ell sexual jokes or make innuendoes.[14]

Many employers are listening, and are in fact enacting broad policies like this.[15] Gone is any safeguard that the "severity or pervasiveness" element of harassment law might provide -- these are programs of zero tolerance for any potentially risky speech. But that is what a cautious employer would do: Because a hostile environment can flow from various little incidents, perpetrated by different people, the employer indeed has to "nip these activities in the bud." Employers have to prohibit each individual joke or cartoon or what have you, because they can never know when the speech will in the aggregate become "severe or pervasive" enough to lead to liability.

Of course, there are other employers who undercensor -- who don't punish even the most egregious behavior. Harassment law, like many laws, is both underenforced and overenforced. The ill-intentioned and ill-counseled employers do little; but other employers are pushed into imposing significant speech restrictions.

"Harassment" Outside the Law

So far I have been talking about the dangers of harassment law. But even outside the law, an overly broad definition of "harassment" has its costs. A sexual harassment allegation is a pretty powerful thing, even if it doesn't come in a lawsuit. If "harassment" is defined to include lots of innocent conduct, that conduct might end up getting people into unwarranted hot water. On the other hand, there's a risk here of crying wolf: As the overbreadth of the definition becomes more notorious, the charge might generally lose its sting, so even genuine harassment might end up becoming harder to condemn.

Consider the findings of a recent "scholarly" report, written by two professors at the University of Dayton and a graduate student, presented at an academic conference, and widely cited in the media.[16] The typical hour of TV sit-coms in 1990, the report says, showed 9 incidents of sexual harassment. And instead of condemning this behavior, the TV programs actually seemed to approve of it. Television, the report concludes, "may actually encourage sexual[ly] harassing actions by failing to portray the unacceptableness of the behaviors."

But what, exactly, did the report mean by "harassment"? Well, here are the categories of conduct that the report covered: sexual remarks; sexually suggestive looks and gestures; kissing; touching or grabbing with sexual intent; date requests; physical space violations with sexual intent. To be harassment the behavior had to be "unwelcome" -- if the conduct "was cordially accepted by the recipient," or if it was "ignored or not heard," it does not qualify.

Under this definition, here is what "harassment" could include:

- John says, "Sue, would you go out with me?" Sue says, "With you? No way!"
- John meets Sue at a bar, talks to her a bit, and tells her, "Baby, you are one hot mama" (this quote is the researchers' own example). Sue says, "Well, actually, I think you are a dweeb."
- John is at a party and looks at Sue suggestively. Sue turns to her friend and asks, "Who is that jerk?"

In fact, over 90 percent of the so-called harassment the researchers found was sexual remarks, sexually suggestive looks and gestures, and requests for dates. Only 5.6 percent of the incidents fell into more serious categories -- unwelcome kissing, touching, or grabbing; another 1.6 percent were "physical space violations." Nearly 95 percent of the conduct occurred outside the workplace.

The great majority of this is certainly not harassment from a legal point of view. The researchers claim they used the "legal definition of sexual harassment," but of course they are wrong. The law does not apply to parties or bars -- it covers only the workplace and, to some extent, the schoolhouse. And, as I mentioned above, to be illegal the conduct must be "severe or pervasive" enough to create a "hostile or abusive" environment. Vague as these terms may be, it's clear that one remark or look or date request does not constitute "harassment."

But even setting aside the law, most of what the researchers describe ranges from the unobjectionable -- sometimes, if you ask someone out, they will say no -- to the merely mildly rude. Maybe some of the remarks, gestures, looks or date requests were indeed harassment: sexual extortion by people in a position of power, or persistent insults or unwanted romantic pursuit. But the Dayton researchers made no effort to separate the real harassment from the spurious.

The Dayton researchers are not alone: "Harassment" is chronically redefined by people to mean whatever suits their theory. A few years ago there was a lot of press about the American Association of University Women's "Hostile Hallways" report. Eighty-five percent of all high school girls and 76 percent of high school boys, the report said, had been sexually harassed in high school.[17]

The problem was that the report defined harassment to cover anyone who has even once, in the four-year hormonal pressure cooker of high school, been the target of any unwanted "sexual comments, jokes, gestures, or looks." Given that, the only surprise is that 20 percent of all high school graduates had never been leered at.

Definitions which lump so much acceptable conduct together with the unacceptable cannot possibly yield useful data. But beyond this, broad definitions of "harassment" reveal a deeply wrongheaded view of the relations between the sexes. Consider one of the Dayton researchers' complaints: TV may give viewers "inaccurate conceptions about the appropriateness of sexually suggestive looks, gestures, and remarks. In this study, these behaviors were frequently portrayed as a favorable and positive way to initiate relationships."

As it happens, sexually suggestive looks sometimes *are* a positive way to initiate a relationship. Humans don't mate through antiseptic exchanges of formal proposals, calculated to avoid the slightest risk of offense. They look, they talk, they flirt. Sometimes they get rejected; sometimes they miscalculate, and come across as vulgar or juvenile. But calling every unwanted date request or sexual look "harassment" betrays a lack of any sense of proportion.

And the fanaticism that it takes to condemn "sexually suggestive looks" as harassment is not easily cabined. The last few sentences of the Dayton report are chilling: "This current study has established that sexual harassment" -- as the authors define it -- "is prevalent in the popular media ... Ultimately, the escalation of this debate will surely test the relationship between the right to free expression and the expectation of socially responsible behavior." The right to free expression is endangered because TV does not condemn rejected suitors, or even mildly vulgar louts.

"Harassment" in the Lecture

Finally, a few examples from a domain on the border of law and social convention: Alleged "harassment" by lecturers in the classroom.

Consider one of the incidents I mentioned in the beginning: To illustrate the concept of intentional act, Graydon Snyder of the Chicago Theological Seminary used a Talmudic story in which a man falls from a roof onto a woman and they accidentally have sex. A student complained this was sexual harassment: "She said," Snyder reported, "that men who have abused her always say that they did not intend to, and in that lecture, I gave support to those men who -- without intending to hurt women -- abuse and hurt them anyway."[18] The school agreed with the student, put Snyder on probation, and told him to take sexual harassment workshops.[19]

Or consider Eastern Illinois University Professor Douglas DiBanco, who was accused of "sexual and cultural harassment" because he "criticized Christianity and discussed phallic symbols and Freudian analyses during music classes."[20] Or Chuck Jorgensen at L.A. Valley College, who was charged by a student with sexual harassment; I quote from the complaint letter:

> I felt I was sexually harassed by a teacher ... One student asked Mr. Jorgensen if he accepted extra credit. Mr. Jorgensen said that he doesn't believe in extra credit. He said that he used to ask for sexual favors as extra credit, but he doesn't do that any more. Not because he doesn't like [it] but because of AIDS. He also used frequently profanity such as the

F___[sic] word. Another thing he talked about was how he had a heart attack and his doctor told him he had to give up five things: fooling around; illicit drugs; hard alcohol; (something else I can't remember) and stress. He then said, "Well, one out of five isn't bad -- so I just don't get stressed as much."[21]

And these are far from the only incidents like this.[22]

Part of the problem in these cases has to do with academic freedom; as a general rule, university professors ought to have broad latitude in deciding what to teach and how to teach it. But I admit this is a complicated issue. Universities must have some rights to control what their professors say in class -- for instance, if the professor strays entirely from the topic, or personally insults his students, the administration should be able to step in and make sure the students get their money's worth. I can even imagine a religious university legitimately asking the instructors to avoid profanity. There is some risk here, but it might often be proper to give the administration latitude to require teaching styles that seem to it more effective or more polite.

The main problem is that characterizing the matter as "harassment" moves things onto an entirely different, and more dangerous, plane. It is one thing to see conduct as an unsound teaching practice, which would usually lead to little more than some talks between the teacher and the administration. It is quite another to call it harassment -- a word laden with connotations of moral turpitude, of invasion of students' rights, of discrimination, of possible violation of federal or state law. Compare the following phrases: "Professor Jorgensen has a vulgar sense of humor, and sometimes swears in class -- the school ought to do something about that." "Professor Jorgensen sexually harasses his students -- the school ought to do something about that." Which would you rather have said about you?

Again, we see the same pattern: A vague, broad definition of sexual harassment; disproportionate outrage at material that ranges from the juvenile to the harmless; and a resulting chill on free expression.

Conclusion

The definition of "harassment" has widened considerably in recent years. Harassment is no longer limited to sexual extortion, physical abuse, or even face-to-face slurs. In the courts, in universities, and in the media, "harassment" now includes a good deal of speech that should be protected by the First Amendment; a good deal of behavior that is peccadillo at most and often not even that; and if one adopts the broadest definitions, a good deal of behavior that is nothing more than the normal, and not remarkably offensive, mating dance of the human animal.

Harassment law and harassment discourse is ripe for an overhaul. Of course, we shouldn't throw the baby out with the bathwater; some of what's called "harassment" is genuinely nasty stuff, and deserves punishment and condemnation. But at the same time, we should remember some basic principles:

1. *Even if you call speech "harassment," it is still speech* -- it is still behavior that the Constitution specifically protects. Some speech restrictions (for instance, restrictions on one-on-one slurs) might be permissible, but a good many other restrictions may not be.

2. *If you cannot define it, do not ban it.* Threatening people with huge liability for allowing speech that is "severe or pervasive" enough to create a "hostile or abusive environment" is asking for trouble. Vague standards like this are recipes for overcensorship, as well as for simple injustice. Especially where speech restrictions are involved, people are entitled to know what the law allows and what it does not.

3. *Sex is not necessarily dirty.* A lot of talk about sex is juvenile, and some of it might indeed be genuinely offensive. But surely a picture of one's wife in a bathing suit and a Talmudic story are within the boundaries of acceptable behavior. The U.S. has a long and, in my view, unhappy tradition of suppressing art, humor, and language that have a sexual component. In the last several decades, we seem to have gotten beyond this puritanism, and I would hate to see the concept of "harassment" erase these gains.

4. *Allegations of "harassment" are often the wrong tool for policing offensiveness or rudeness.* People who have to live together should try to accommodate each other's foibles. Sometimes listeners should keep quiet about speech they find offensive; sometimes speakers should stop saying things even if they think the listeners' objections are unreasonable. But a charge of "sexual harassment," with all the baggage the term now carries, is much too big a gun here. Talking in terms of politeness, accommodation, maturity, or effective communication may be more productive than talking sexism or harassment or discrimination.

End Notes

1. 42 U.S.C. §2000e-2(a)(1).

2. *Harris v. Forklift Systems, Inc.*, 114 S. Ct. 367, 370 (1993); *Eggleston v. South Bend Community School Corp.*, 858 F. Supp. 841, 847-48 (N.D. Ind. 1994).

3. *Brown Transp. Corp. v. Commonwealth*, 578 A.2d 555, 562 (Pa. Commw. Ct. 1990) (plaintiff won).

4. *Bowman v. Heller*, 1993 WL 761159 (Mass. Super. Ct. 1993) (verdict for plaintiff of $35,000 plus costs and attorney's fees). On appeal, the Massachusetts Supreme Judicial Court held that this was not harassment, but this holding was based on a state law technicality; it seems quite likely that the finding of harassment would have been upheld had the suit been brought under federal law.

5. *In re* Sapp's Realty, Or. Comm'r of Bureau of Labor & Indus., Case No. 11-83, at 4-748, 66-68, 71 (Jan. 31, 1985) (plaintiff won harassment claim and got money damages).

6. *Tunis v. Corning Glass Works*, 747 F. Supp. 951 (S.D.N.Y. 1990), *aff'd without opinion*, 930 F.2d 910 (2d Cir. 1991). The court here held for the defendant employer, but only because the employer took prompt action to remedy the situation; the judge strongly implied that an employer which continued to let its employees use gender-based language could be liable.

7. Andrew Wolfson, "All Worked Up . . . Phone Company Called to Task Over Gender-Biased Signs," *Louisville Court Journal*, March 3, 1994 at 1B.

8. *Pakizegi v. First National Bank*, 831 F. Supp. 901, 908-09 (D. Mass. 1993) (dictum, ultimately holding for the employer because all offensive conduct was promptly remedied).

9. *Cardin v. Via Tropical Fruits, Inc.*, 1993 U.S. Dist. LEXIS 16302, at *24-*26 & n.4 (S.D. Fla.). The case involved some other, more egregious, conduct, but the court specifically held that "every incident reported by the [plaintiff]" -- the jokes as well as the other conduct -- "involves sexual harassment." *Id.* At *45-*46.

10. Of course, employers have pretty broad powers (for private employers, almost unlimited) to restrict their employees' speech. The First Amendment limits the government, not private employers. But when an employer censors because of the threat of harassment law, that's not just a private decision -- it is the government restricting speech.

11. For a more detailed discussion of these issues, see Eugene Volokh, Comment, "Freedom of Speech and Workplace Harassment," 39 *UCLA L. Rev.* 1791 (1992); Eugene Volokh, "How Harassment Law Restricts Free Speech," 47 *Rutgers Law Review*, 563 (1995); Eugene Volokh, "Freedom of Speech Appellate Review in Workplace Harassment Cases", 90 *Northwestern University Law Review*, 1009 (1996). For a contrary position, which argues that harassment law poses no free speech problems, see Suzanne Sangree, "Title VII Prohibitions Against Hostile Environment Sexual Harassment and the First Amendment: No Collision in Sight", 47 *Rutgers Law Review*, 461 (1995); Suzanne Sangree, "A Reply to Professors Volokh and Browne," 47 *Rutgers Law Review*, 595 (1995). For an argument that even restrictions on face-to-face slurs should generally be unconstitutional (a more speech-protective argument than I make), see Kingsley R. Browne, "Title VII as Censorship: Hostile-Environment Harassment and the First Amendment," 52 *Ohio State Law Journal*, 481 (1991); Kingsley R. Browne, "Workplace Censorship: A Response to Professor Sangree," 47 *Rutgers Law Review*, 579 (1995).

12. *See, e.g.,* 2 *People For the American Way, Artistic Freedom Under Attack* 29, 50, 92, 156, 214, 221 (1994) (listing some similar incidents).

13. Nat Hentoff, "Trivializing Sexual Harassment," *Washington Post*, Jan. 11, 1992, at A19.

14. Phillip M. Perry, "Avoid Costly Lawsuits for Sexual Harassment," *Law Practice Management*, Apr. 1992, at 18, 20, 24.

15. See, e.g., Rosalind Rossi, "Sexual Harassment Ban Spelled Out," *Chicago Sun-Times*, June 23, 1994, at 20.

16. The report is Thomas Skill, James Robinson & Colleen Kinsella, "Sexual Harassment in Network Television Situation Comedies: An Empirical Content Analysis of Fictional Programming One Year Prior to the Clarence Thomas Senate Confirmation

Hearings for the U.S. Supreme Court," a paper presented to the Mass Communication Division of the Speech Communication Association November 1994 National Meeting in New Orleans. For stories citing it, see among many others, Ginny Holbert, "Hotbed of Harassment; Sitcom Sex Comments Are No Joke, Study Says," *Chicago Sun-Times*, Nov. 30, 1994 at 51; Alan Bash, Donna Gable & Jefferson Graham, "Comedies Often Treat Sexual Harassment Lightly," *USA Today*, Nov. 16, 1994, at 3D.

17. See, e.g., Mary Jordan, "Sex Harassment Complaints Starting in Grade School," *Washington Post*, June 2, 1993, at A1.

18. Nat Hentoff, "A Sexual Harasser from the Middle Ages," *Village Voice*, July 26, 1994, at 18.

19. Adriene Drell, "Bible Scholar Sues to Fight Taint of Sex Harassment," *Chicago Sun-Times*, March 25, 1994, at 5.

20. "Prof Defends Religious, Sexual Remarks," *Chicago Sun-Times*, Dec. 1, 1993, at 24.

21. Copy of complaint letter, on file with the author.

22. See, e.g., *Silva v. University of New Hampshire*, 888 F. Supp. 293 (D.N.H. 1994) (professor suspended for a year without pay based primarily on two in-class sexually suggestive analogies; the court reversed this on free speech grounds); *Cohen v. San Bernardino Valley College*, 883 F. Supp. 1407 (C.D. Cal. 1995) (professor disciplined based primarily on in-class remarks; the court affirmed this, concluding the remarks could create a sexually hostile educational environment).

Domestic Violence as a Professional Commitment

David H. Gremillion, Associate Professor of Medicine
University of North Carolina School of Medicine at Chapel Hill

There are many pathways to awareness and involvement in domestic violence issues. Each of these produces a unique set of insights which add to the aggregate knowledge, but also biases which risk fragmenting the effort and creating discord among potential allies. Although we all seek the elimination of violence from families we vigorously cling to our own biases and our dialogue often becomes mired in political and ideological issues. Our perspectives are often shaped by our past, gender, religion or politics. Like the proverbial "blind men describing an elephant" we each feel the anatomy closest to us and "see" a narrowly accurate but incomplete picture of a massive problem.

For many, a personal history of prior abuse is the catalyst leading to a commitment. Individuals who act as volunteers, community representatives and committee members are often self-described "survivors." Their awakening to the issue followed a traumatic event which helped them remove their "blinders" to the issues and simultaneously energized them with a righteous indignation. Such individuals make up a majority of those who work on domestic violence at a grassroots or community level. The domestic violence movement thrives on their zeal and dedication and we owe much to their efforts at a time when it was both unpopular and difficult to be involved. As a result of their experiences they bring valuable insights and skills to the movement. They also frequently bring biases which may prevent them from acknowledging the full spectrum of this complex issue. They frequently focus on the tragic outcomes of domestic violence rather than the processes which lead to that violence and which may be amenable to prevention. To many of them the female victim-male perpetrator model of domestic violence is the only one considered worthy of policy or funding support. Rarely do they note that male victims and female perpetrators exist.

In recent years professional programs in sociology, psychology, women's studies and others have produced a new category of well-educated practitioners and academics whose careers are focused on advocacy, victim services and public awareness campaigns. What they lack in personal experience they make up in ideological fervor. Newcomers to the field quickly learn that their academic authority, ideology, and literary and scholarly skills are blended and that their published works often have content which may be interpreted by outsiders as political commentary, obfuscation or inaccuracies by traditional standards.

Health Care Professionals as "Newcomers"

Health care professionals are latecomers to the field of domestic violence.

Nurses have displayed a greater and earlier involvement than physicians and their literature begins closer to the grass roots movement and is more comprehensive than that of physicians. In the past physicians were resented as insensitive and non-responsive and occasionally were vilified as a major part of the problem, either as perpetrators or as distracted uninvolved professionals. Such characterizations often served to drive physicians away and incite in them a wariness of the political dimensions of the issue. In recent years however, physicians have used their influence in the public forum as well as in their confidential relationships with patients to create a better understanding and improved responsiveness. This involvement has met with a mixed response from the traditional activists and practitioners who feel threatened and fear a diminishing of their roles and perspectives.

My personal involvement derives from observations in my clinical practice of Infectious Diseases. Many of my HIV-positive patients are abused by partners or have experienced abuse and discrimination by others. As a result of this unique pathway my concern initially centered on male victims. This initial awareness of males as victims in a small and historically ostracized group led to a greater awareness of males as DV victims in general. My reading quickly led me to a broader understanding and a realization that violence in the home is one of the most significant issues of our time. Through my reading I learned that the field is dominated by emotion, politics, and poor research. This poor research, coupled with the polarizing effect of some groups, risks loss of objectivity and creates a potential for formulation of bad public policy. This has inevitably led me to greater involvement in domestic violence issues: initially with the North Carolina State Medical Society and subsequently with the Governor's Crime Commission for the State of North Carolina with service on the Violence Against Women committee.

I view my role as providing a balancing force by bringing objectivity and careful data analysis to the deliberations. In speaking of men as abuse victims I do not seek to minimize the even greater impact that abuse has on women. Instead I seek to preserve the involvement of men as problem solvers rather than risk driving them away by declaring them the problem simply because of their gender.

Physicians who are drawn to domestic violence perceive it as a public health issue with certain medical consequences and preventable health care expenditures. The other dimensions to this issue are no less real but are a less immediate concern to the still male-dominated medical profession. To many activists domestic violence is a small piece of a broader political struggle focused on gender issues and the feminist tradition. This is concerning to many physicians who fear losing the sanctity of their patient relationships and colleague support if they become too closely identified with the controversial aspects of the issue.

Physicians who choose to become involved may face a torrent of scrutiny and at times scorn as their involvement is interpreted by others in the context of these broader social and political issues. Physicians who associate with stigmatized or victimized populations are often viewed with suspicion by their colleagues. This scorn is often by colleagues or others active in the field and for me personally has taken the form of derogatory private and public comments, harassing calls, negative communication to my superiors and colleagues, and inappropriate and obsequious attempts to change language in proposed publications. Negative reaction to non-traditionalists who refuse to "tow the party line" is nothing new. Reports by Straus, Jacobson and others identify dangers inherent in authoring critical analyses.[1]

Most physicians are poorly prepared to deal with domestic violence issues and even when properly motivated face a daunting spectrum of barriers[2] (Table 1). This poor preparation may produce risky and embarrassing missteps which, although taken in good faith, become fodder for their omnipresent critics. Nevertheless, when they get involved they are perceived as among the most helpful.[3]

Table 1 Factors Limiting Physician Involvement in Domestic Violence

Professional Factors	*Institutional and Legal Factors*
Time constraints	Fear of legal reprisal
Inadequate skills	Limited institutional resources
Professional relationship with abuser	Inadequate or unclear policies
Professional "detachment"	Loss of insurance
Gender bias	
Personal history of abuse	

The new entrants to the field have provoked some tension and anxiety among traditional practitioners and activists in the field. The volunteers who were so instrumental in developing programs and shelter movements are concerned that "professionalization" or "medicalization" of the field will exclude their grassroots insight and zeal. The evolution of the domestic violence movement and the foundation for these tensions is reviewed by Hazelwood and Shupe in their recent book *Violent Couples*.[4]

Problems with Domestic Violence Literature

One of the first problems that physicians face is the disordered nature of the professional publication in the field. The published literature on domestic violence is very diffuse, eclectic and confused. Searching the literature for relevant articles is challenging since the number of search terms is large (Table 2).

Table 2   Search Terms in Major Medical Databases

Domestic violence	Women
Battering	Elder Abuse
Spouse abuse	Batterers
Family violence	Battered women

The confusion in the scientific literature results partly from the diversity of search terms and the scattered and at times inaccessible journals. If a newcomer to the field assumes that "battered woman" is equivalent to "domestic violence" and carries this assumption into the selection of search terms for one of the major databases they will miss approximately 98% of published literature. Moreover, the scope of their search will not only be quantitatively restricted but qualitatively restricted by the bias inherent in equating the two terms. The search term "battered woman" is not accompanied by its logical corollary "battered man" in spite of solid documentation that battering of males by either male or female partners is a substantial issue.[5] This is a search logic flaw which excludes all but women victims. Search terms may not overlap between the major medical databases.[6] For instance, CINHAL lists 121 citations from 1982 - 1995 for the search term domestic violence. For family violence, there are 236 citations. In contrast MEDLINE lists 444 and 210 respectively. PSYCHLIT is another database which shows some disparity in citations (Table 3). The term "spouse abuse" has been used in recent years, as has "battered woman," with varied representations in the different data bases.

Table 3   Number of citations by search term and database, 1982-1995

Database	Domestic Violence	Family Violence	Spouse Abuse	Battered Women
MEDLINE	444	210	1099	27
CINHAL	121	236	339	41
PSYCHLIT	332	1144	156	51

The quality of published literature leaves much to be desired. Many publications show little evidence of editorial oversight or scrutiny and are frequently laced with political commentary (Table 4) or have improper conclusions based on the data presented. The political commentary is disturbing to physicians even though some of the most inflammatory passages occasionally are by MDs.

Table 4 Selected Examples of Political Commentary

"The use of patriarchal logic by medical providers ostensibly responding to physical trauma has less to do with individual 'sexism' than with the political and economic constraints under which medicine operates as part of an 'extended patriarchy' ... serves to reconstitute the 'private world' of patriarchial authority with violence if necessary, against demands to socialize the labor of love."
"Medicine must align its structure, procedures, and ideology with the overall structure of domination in a bourgeois society."
Int. J. Health Serv. 1979; 9 (3): 461-93. Dr. Anne Flitcraft, MD
"Here presented are the facts, stripped of the distortions of a male dominated profession."
Nebr Med J 1993, March; 78 (3): 52-8.

I was surprised to find one of the AMA's major advisors on the issue caught up in "capitalist and bourgeois" rhetoric and discussions of "suppression of the underclass by the surrogate patriarchy of medicine." Such commentary in medical literature is clearly a "turn off" for physicians who, although concerned about domestic violence, are less inclined to translate that concern into social and political activism.

There are relatively few population based studies and these are available only in non-mainstream journals. Most studies are based narrowly on the examinations of shelter populations or evaluations of batterers identified through them. Research limited only to such self-identified "at risk" populations would not be tolerated in other areas of scholarly inquiry. Such studies unfortunately present one-sided views of a very complex issue. Research on batterers is narrowly focused and rarely presents a comparison with normal males. This apparently relates to the prevailing view that there are no "normal males"[7] as much as it does to poor design. This research assumes that battering is a fundamental aspect of maleness rather than a pathology which is potentially amenable to correction. Much research, however, clearly shows that there is an increased incidence in substance abuse and certain personality disorders among batterers. By disallowing pathology or addictive behaviors to be partly responsible, some advocacy researchers are able to declare that maleness itself is the pathology.

The obscurity and inaccessibility of some journal titles limits the scope of a scholar's review. Of the 575 citations in the major databases for calendar years 1994 and 1995, over 75% were in journals which are not readily available in most medical libraries. Furthermore, only 15% of citations were in journals routinely available to or reviewed by practicing physicians. These database issues are more than just arcane academic hurdles for scholars; they have practical impact and can produce inaccurate research and bad public policy. For instance, a casual researcher in the field would not routinely recover such landmark articles as Straus and Gelles' population based surveys,[8] McNeely's critical editorial,[9] or Susan Steinmetz's article on the "battered male."[10] A careful review of all of the major databases using multiple search terms and strategies fails to display any of these critical titles and would leave the casual researcher with a limited view. Media representations of social research in domestic violence is often inaccurate or biased, thus further discrediting published literature.[11] Dr. Sommers has recently reviewed many instances of research obfuscation and public news accountings by activists.[12] Their intentions may be good but in the long run they serve to discredit the field and drive away potential problem solvers.

We should not be surprised at the diversity of opinion and occasional conflict among workers in the domestic violence field. Our backgrounds, biases and even bodies of knowledge are often quite different. The movement is growing past this fragmented stage of its development. Now professionals with a more balanced and mainstream vision are adding to the significant contributions of others. Better access to information and databases as well as careful editorial oversight are limiting the amount of "advocacy research" that is being published. This will eventually pay dividends in better public policy and support programs. Our goals must remain simple: to reduce abusive and violent behaviors by all family members, rather than to exploit the political or ideological vulnerabilities created in the context of this issue. This alone will keep the medical profession fully committed to its role in domestic violence.

End Notes

1. Jacobson, N.S. "Rewards and Dangers in Researching Domestic Violence." *Family Process*, 1994, 33:81-85.
2. Gremillion, D.H., Evins, G. "Why Don't Doctors Identify and Refer Victims of Domestic Violence?" *North Carolina Medical Journal*, 1994, 55:428-433.
3. Hamilton, B., and Coates, J. "Perceived Helpfulness and Use of Professional Services by Abused Women." *Journal of Family Violence*, 8 (4), 1993.
4. Stacey, W.A., Hazlewood, L.R., Shupe A. *The Violent Couple*. Praeger, 1994:16-30.
5. Straus, M.A. "Physical Assaults by Wives: a Major Social Problem." In: Gelles, R.J., Loseke, D.R., eds. *Current Controversies on Family Violence*. Newbury Park, CA: Sage, 1993:67-87.
6. Major Medical Databases: *MEDLINE* (R) is the bibliographic database of the National Library of Medicine containing references to articles from more than 3700 journals; *PSYCHLIT Database* (R) contains summaries of the world's literature in psychology and related disciplines and is compiled from the PsycINFO Database. PSYCHLIT covers over 1300 journals in 27 languages from approximately 50 countries; *CINHAL* (R) is the most widely used index for English language nursing journals, and 13 allied health disciplines.

7. Holtzworth-Munroe, A., Waltz, J., Jacobson, N.S., Monaco, V., Fehrenbach, P.A., Gottman, J.M. "Recruiting Nonviolent Men as Control Subjects For Research on Marital Violence: How Easily Can it be Done?" *Violence,* 1992, Spring 7(1):79-88.

8. Publications by Murray Straus and colleagues: Straus, M.A. "Physical Assaults by Wives: A Major Social Problem." In: Gelles, R.J., Loseke, D.R., eds. *Current Controversies on Family Violence.* Newbury Park, CA: Sage, 1993:67-87; Straus M.A., Gelles R.J. "Societal Change and Change in Family Violence from 1975 to 1985 As Revealed by Two National Surveys." *Journal of Marriage and the Family* 1986, 48:465-79; Straus, M.A., Cantor, G.K. "Change In Spouse Assault Rates From 1975 to 1992: A Comparison of Three National Surveys in the United States." 13th World Congress of Sociology 1994; July 14, 1994, Bitburg, Germany; Straus, M.A., Kantor, B.K. "Change in Cultural Norms Approving Marital Violence from 1968 to 1994." Presented to the Bitburg conference, 1994.; Stets, J.E., Straus, M.A. "Gender Differences in Reporting Marital Violence and Its Medical and Psychological Consequences." In *Physical Violence in American Families.* Transaction Books, 1990.

9. McNeely, R.L., Robinson-Simpson, G. "The Truth About Domestic Violence: A Falsely Framed Issue." *Social Work,* 1987 Nov.-Dec., Vol 32 (6):485-90.

10. Steinmetz, S.K. "The Battered Husband Syndrome." *Victimology,* 1977, 2:499-509.

11. Angell, M., Kassirer, J.P. "Clinical Research -- What Should the Public Believe?" *New England Journal of Medicine,* 1994, 331:189-190.

12. Sommers, C.H. *Who Stole Feminism?* New York: Simon and Schuster, 1994: 189-208.

Controversy Within Family Violence Research

Reena Sommer, Assistant Professor
Department of Community Health Services,
University of Manitoba, Canada

I have been involved in the study of partner abuse for the past eight years. My interest in this issue began with my concern about violence against women. Initially, my examination of partner abuse focused on courtship violence and spouse abuse perpetrated by men. My sense of curiosity led me to go against what I believed to be the essence of partner abuse and examine the prevalence of abuse perpetrated by women. Quite to my surprise, I found that women, too, abused their male partners at equivalent rates. This led me to search out other research examining this issue, and again to my surprise I found my findings were not an anomaly, but had considerable support.

Considerable controversy has emerged as a result of studies finding equivalent rates of abuse for males and females. The rift within family violence research centers on how researchers have approached their investigations. On one hand, there is the unidimensional approach to partner abuse advanced by feminists. They view abuse between intimates as a problem of women being abused by men whereby the abuse is perceived as a dichotomous variable (abuse/no abuse) and seen in its most severe forms. On the other hand, sociologists and family researchers view partner abuse as being gender neutral and occurring along a continuum with no abuse at one end and very severe abuse at the other end.

I would like to address this controversy by first providing a backdrop to how the divisiveness in the study of partner abuse developed, and then by discussing some of the methodological and practical issues that have contributed to it.

Long before the first reference to violence within the family was made in academic circles -- which was actually not that long ago, somewhere around 32 years ago -- the goings on within the family took on a very different tenor than they do today. Back then, family problems were considered private and were no one's business but those directly involved. This is not to say that the outside world was totally oblivious to the problems that some families experienced. On the contrary, family problems were often quite apparent; however, they were defined somewhat differently and were viewed as issues that were to be resolved without outside interference.

I'm sure those of us old enough to remember those simpler times will recall stories about families whose children went to school unclean and inadequately fed or clothed. There were also stories about husbands and wives who quarrelled a little too much, and whose houses echoed with sounds of yelling and items hitting the walls. We may recall husbands who were labelled as boors, and wives who were labelled as henpeckers because they didn't treat their respective spouses with the respect or consideration we thought they deserved. We may also recall stories of elderly people stranded in their homes, unable to adequately care for themselves while their able children came only rarely to visit and did so just for a few minutes. I would venture to suggest that back then, we would not have considered these as examples of abuse by today's standards. Instead, we probably thought about how unfortunate these families were and how thankful we were that such things did not go on in our own families.

The explosion of research in family violence as well as the work done by the women's movement has not only redefined how we look at family violence, but also how we approach family issues, in general. During the past three decades, the family has been placed under the social science microscope and has been examined in many different ways. We have learned about the division of labour within households, different child rearing practices, and alternative lifestyles, to name just a few. What was once considered a troublesome but private problem is now defined as abuse in its various forms and is subject to the scrutiny of numerous social agencies. In the case of family violence, this move toward deprivatizing the family has been positive in many respects and has led to the protection of those unable to protect themselves. Today, we have very strict guidelines about the reporting and handling of child abuse cases and legislation concerning protecting the elderly is currently in place in many U.S. states and Canadian provinces.

Twenty-five years ago, the problem of wife abuse went virtually unnoticed by the legal, medical, social and research communities. Then, women caught in abusive relationships were left to suffer in silence with nowhere to turn to for help or understanding. Little support was provided by their own families because of strong adherence to the notion of "'til death do you part." Much of the credit for the increased public knowledge about wife assaults is attributed to the women's movement which, through its tireless efforts, has brought the issue of wife battering to the forefront. Today, wife abuse has been identified as the single most important dimension of family violence. In fact, lobbying efforts by women's groups have been so successful that the issue of wife abuse has taken precedence over other social problems such as poverty, alcoholism, and unemployment as well as the more pressing medical problem of breast cancer, which affects one in eight American women.

With all it has accomplished, the lobby for the protection of women has been at the expense of protecting other family members also at risk for abuse. In some quarters of both popular and media cultures, as well as the legislative culture, violence against women by men has literally squeezed out recognition of other forms of family violence, including the violence perpetrated by women against other women (siblings, daughters, mothers and lesbian partners), against children, and indeed against male partners and elderly fathers. Especially noteworthy is research which reports that female perpetrators commit between 3% and 13% of all sexual abuse. The tunnel vision view of domestic violence where women are the victims and men are the perpetrators is built on the patriarchal model which conceptualizes abuse as resulting from men's overt attempts to dominate women. This conceptual framework argues that men are socialized into violence, and is supported by many of our social institutions, most notably the institution of marriage. Feminist writers maintain that violence by men is pervasive and normal, and some have gone as far as to equate violence against women with jungle warfare.

At the center of the debate on family violence is the argument over who is the biggest victim. Feminists would have us believe that women are unquestionably the greater victims and men are the greater perpetrators -- even at the cost of invented figures, illogical arguments and suppressed empirical data which dispel this position. It has been suggested that feminists fear that what is perceived as the more serious problem of wife abuse will be impeded by drawing attention to other forms of domestic violence. In other words, it is believed that by sharing the victim spotlight with men, funds will be diverted away from women's shelters and advocacy and toward the needs of men and others suffering abuse. Is it too naive of me to suggest that by viewing family violence -- and specifically spouse abuse -- as a much larger problem than it has been until now, more funds could be directed to domestic abuse programs which recognize the role of both partners? These funds could then be used to bring about long term solutions by working with couples and their families instead of the current band aid strategies that shelters offer to women alone.

It is only recently that the presentation of domestic abuse as solely a matter of the victimization of women by men has begun to be questioned by academics, government officials, the media and the public. More and more often, stories about women assaulting their family members appear in our newspapers. Although the story of Susan Smith shocked the nation, a perusal of newspaper articles reveals that she is not the first woman to harm her children. Still, examples of women's violence are continually dismissed as rare events while examples of violence by men are held as symbols of their innate violent make-up. As a consequence, challenges to the patriarchal model of spouse abuse have not been well-received by women's advocates, and in fact have been labelled as the "backlash" in the violence against women struggle.

The controversy over the salience of the feminist stance on wife assault has been discussed by only a few academics. The penalties against criticizing feminist ideology are varied, but nevertheless severe. They range from personal attacks, such as name-calling and malicious rumours, to threats to academic careers, to threats to their family members. Because of this, many academics feel the price of speaking out is too high to pay. On the other hand, those who have braved the consequences and spoken out have gained public attention and given many reason to rethink what have till now become accepted truths in our societal consciousness. Those who have dared to question the myopic, unidimensional view of domestic abuse have done so because of their commitment to see that the issue of violence perpetrated by women is brought to the forefront after being hidden, as wife abuse was 20 years ago.

While there is no shortage of official statistics, emergency room reports, and anecdotes from shelters supporting the claim that women are very often severely abused by their male partners, these claims in no way: 1) describe the condition of all women in society, nor 2) do they address the issue of abuse sustained by men that has already been demonstrated by several large general population surveys.

With respect to my first point concerning the generalizing of findings from one population to another, I will begin by stating that we must remember that the cases that are described by these clinical data sources (that is, the shelters, police and hospitals) reflect the tail end of domestic abuse cases. In other words, these are the most serious examples of domestic abuse. On the other hand, surveys conducted on random samples of men and women in the general population find equivalent rates of abuse in which the abuse is, relatively speaking, more benign in nature. By that I mean, the tactics used during incidents of abuse have a lower probability of producing injuries. This is supported by the low rates of injuries reported.

Much of the confusion in the debate over whether or not women are the sole victims of male-perpetrated abuse centers around the data source used to report cases of abuse. To resolve this debate, we must begin by asking, "Why do women overshadow men in cases of severe abuse?" Based on the information that has flooded the media, the most obvious answer would be "because that is the way it is; these statistics reflect reality." However, there is an alternative explanation, which is: "Women overshadow men in reports of severe domestic abuse because the sources from which we gather data do not adequately reflect cases of abused males." Think about it, how many abused men can we expect to find in battered women's shelters?

You might argue, though, that police and emergency room statistics have likewise failed to produce large numbers of male victims of domestic abuse. How do I explain that? My answer is, "Look at the cities that have instituted zero tolerance domestic abuse policies." If you compare pre-policy male/female arrest ratios with those at present, you will undoubtedly find that the gap between male/female arrests is quickly closing. In fact, in my hometown of Winnipeg, Manitoba, the number of arrests of females is escalating faster than the number of arrests of males. Unfortunately, data on emergency rooms is not as convincing, in that few men report domestic abuse as the cause of their injuries. However, based on the anecdotal reports of injured men, many say they often lie because they fear they will not be believed.

The bottom line is, we do not have a comparable clinical population of abused men. Appropriate comparisons cannot yet be made between clinically abused males and females, nor can the issue of injuries sustained be appropriately addressed without a parallel population of abused men. Until such time, the motivations for the abuse as well as its associated factors within this high risk population remain unresolved. For now, valid comparisons of male and female abusers should be limited to research conducted on either random samples from the general population or convenience samples drawn from a number of sources, including therapy groups. Unfortunately, this is something that is rarely done and is certainly not reflected in media reports.

In terms of my other point concerning the abuse sustained by men, I will say again, there is ample empirical evidence demonstrating that the perpetration and victimization of spousal abuse within the general population is shared by both men and women. Spousal abuse is not exclusively a women's issue. Yet this notion of domestic violence as being solely a women's issue still persists. In addition to what has already been said, the strong adherence to female victimization by males centers on women's use of violence as being motivated only by self-defence as well as men's greater relative physical strength over women.

Research by Straus and colleagues has demonstrated that an equal proportion of men and women initiate episodes of domestic abuse. This suggests that self-defence is not likely a factor in these cases. My own research goes a step further by straightforwardly asking "Was the abuse perpetrated in self-defense?" Results indicated that only 9.9% of women and 14.8% of men said they perpetrated abuse in self-defence during the year prior to the survey. In other words, for the vast majority of men and women, the abuse they perpetrated was for reasons other than self-defence.

To date, there are no data that take into account height and weight as a factor involved in the perpetration of domestic abuse. As a result, comments regarding men's greater relative physical strength as a predictor of perpetrated abuse are strictly speculative. While it makes intuitive sense that a person of greater stature and strength will have the advantage in a physical assault, it would be a mistake to believe that one's greater relative strength is the only determining factor in the outcome of a domestic assault. Anecdotal reports from abused men suggest that small-framed women exert considerable fear and intimidation by threatening to take their children away and by other forms of emotional abuse such as insults and degradation. We know all too well that anyone can compensate for a lack of strength with a weapon. The case of Lorena and John Bobbitt speaks to that issue quite well.

My point is that we should not automatically jump onto the bandwagon that discredits the other reality that men, like women, can be victims as well as perpetrators of abuse. Regardless of our gender, we are all members of the same human species with the same innate drives of flight or fight. Each one of us has the ability to react violently given the right set of circumstances. What the literature on spousal abuse has shown us is that there is considerable variability in what triggers violent responses to marital conflicts. Some abusers are triggered by stress, while others are triggered by alcohol, unemployment, family background or poor coping skills. In most cases, it is a complex combination and interaction of these factors that predispose men and women to use violence to resolve conflicts in their intimate relationships. The job of research is to identify these triggers and be able to accurately predict who is most vulnerable and under what set of circumstances. Once accomplished, the road to effective intervention may be at hand.

As a woman who is deeply concerned about the well-being of all women, I cannot help being frustrated by attempts to resolve the abuse that many women suffer by turning a blind eye to other women who inflict serious physical and emotional abuse on their loved ones. By denying this aspect of many women's existence, we do little to help women cope with life's stressors, or assist them in building more satisfactory intimate relationships. In our efforts to improve the lives of all women, it is incumbent upon us to see all aspects of their reality. Even more damaging to the image of women is the self-imposed label of victim. In doing so, we deny ourselves the empowerment that we have long strived toward. As long as women subscribe to the notion of universal victimhood, they will never experience the freedom that goes along with having control over their lives.

The truth is we are not all victims. Research shows us that 89% to 97% of couples reported no violence during the year prior to the surveys conducted. In light of these findings, it seems that it would be more appropriate to examine the factors associated with women who have risen above the abuse and have made positive changes in their lives instead of continuously focusing on the small subset of women who have been unable to free themselves from extremely violent relationships. An approach such as this may provide the needed insight to help those still caught in abusive relationships. If not for ourselves, then we need to think about our children and do what is necessary to improve their lives. Since domestic abuse is often handed down from one generation to the next, the only way we can protect our children's future is to stop the abuse they witness and experience in their lives today. Let's take off our politically correct blinders and see the problem of domestic violence for what it really is. Domestic abuse involves and affects all family members!

Family Violence: The Role of Abusive Mothers

The Honorable Anne C. Cools, Senator
Senate of Canada

An enormous advance in family aggression was enabled by the use of radiology, x-ray technology. In 1946, an American, Dr. John Caffey, boldly declared his observations regarding the association between subdural hematoma and abnormal x-ray changes in the long bones of children, stating that these trauma were not accidental, but were willfully inflicted. These two revelations caused much shock and reaction. This questioning of children's injuries was continued by an American, Dr. Frederic Silverman. These modern investigations culminated in the work of another American, Dr. Henry Kempe, who created the term *the battered child syndrome* in 1961.[1] One hundred years prior, Dr. Ambroise Tardieu's work in forensic medicine at the Paris morgue in France resulted in his conclusion that these children had suffered greatly at the hands of their parents and that their injuries did not match the parents' account. In 1860, he published the following:

> . . . those defenseless unfortunate children . . .that their lives, hardly begun, should be nothing but a long agony, . . . tortures before which even our imagination recoils in horror, should consume their bodies . . . shorten their lives, and finally, the most unbelievable thing of all, that the executioners of these children should be more often than not the very people who gave them life . . . This is one of the most terrifying problems that can trouble the heart of man.[2]

The journey from Dr. Tardieu to Dr. Kempe took one hundred years. Now a new journey is beginning; that journey is the examination of feminine aggression and its impact in the family, and its social consequences.

In 1977, Toronto and Ontario were horrified by the child abuse neglect (CAN) death of one month old Vicky Starr Ellis. But for the initiative of the Coroner, Dr. Elie Cass, this death would have passed unnoticed, as do many children's deaths. A five week inquest was held costing over $2,000,000.00. The mother, Deborah Ellis, is a textbook case of an abused child becoming an abusing parent. Deborah had grown up brutally abused by the women in her life, by her mother and her grandmother. In all, Deborah Ellis had six children, sired by six different men. Of these six, three died at her hands, and a fourth nearly died. Parrish, at seventeen months, drowned unattended in the bathtub; Darlene, age eleven months, died of neglect; and Vicky Starr, barely one month old, also died of neglect; Charlene, age two years, was rescued 15 minutes from death by an able medical response. Three children were apprehended, including her sixth, who was apprehended at birth. In his book *Who Speaks for the Children?* author Peter Silverman describes the father of little Vicky Starr as a man who:

> . . . was dominated by his wife. A man described as having only a grade
> two education, semiliterate and of a lower than average intelligence, with
> suicidal tendencies, he shared with his wife a childhood of abuse . . . he
> was badly mistreated by his stepfathers.[3]

Dr. Badari Rickhi, a psychiatrist at Toronto Western Hospital, described this
conjugal relationship as:

> . . . One of the sado-masochistic type, in which the wife and her lovers
> flaunt their affairs before him [the husband] or the wife beats him up,
> which he accepts passively saying that he loves his wife."[4]

Part of Deborah Ellis' disorder was her compulsion to have children. She once said
that:

> No one can stop me having children -- not the judge, or the coroner, or the
> Children's Aid Society.[5]

Dr. Clive Chamberlain, then Director of the Family Court Clinic, wrote:

> Since part of Mrs. Ellis' personality disorder was a compulsion to have
> children, and since nothing could be done to prevent it, she should have
> another chance, through Vicky, to learn how to mother for the sake of
> children yet unborn.[6]

Little Vicky's life was to be an educational tool for Deborah Ellis, whose life was
a tangle of pathologies. Within a month of Vicky Ellis' return to her mother's care,
she was dead.

In Chantham, New Brunswick, a trial has just been completed of a mother and
father in the CAN death of their three year old son, John Ryan Turner, who was
brutally beaten, starved, and kept in a harness, with a gag in his mouth to inhibit
crying. At death he weighed 21 pounds, well below the 32 pound average weight
of a three year old.

In British Columbia, the judicial inquiry by Judge Thomas Gove into the death
of five year old Matthew Vaudreuil is continuing. Matthew suffered beatings at the
hands of his mother, Vera Vaudreuil, including one which broke nine of his ribs
before the final, lethal one that killed him. For this, Vera Vaudreuil is serving a
four year prison term. There were 60 protection reports about Matthew Vaudreuil;
the first one was written the day he was born, and the sixtieth just two days before
his death.[7] Matthew had been seen by health professionals at least 48 times, and
Matthew and his mother had received the services of financial aid workers, home
support workers, mental health workers, public health nurses, psychologists, foster
parents, and 16 child protection workers over the course of five years.[8] Matthew

Vaudreuil's history of maternal neglect and abuse was well known, and yet, he died.

Dr. Cyril Greenland has studied the matter of child abuse neglect deaths. In 1986, he examined and analyzed the records of one hundred child abuse neglect deaths, from 1973 to 1982 in Ontario. These records were from the Chief Coroner's Office. Dr. Greenland reported in an article entitled "Preventing Child Abuse and Neglect Deaths: Identification and Management of High Risk Cases" that:

> The risk of death due to CAN is highest in the first year of life. The Ontario data, confirmed by most other studies, show that well over half of the victims, . . . died before the age of 12 months. An additional 25% died before the age of two years. Only five percent of the victims were over the age of five years.[9]

About the perpetrators, Dr. Greenland noted:

> Natural parents were the perpetrators in 63% of the deaths; mothers were involved in 38 deaths, fathers in 13 deaths and both parents in 12 deaths.[10]

Statistics Canada, in its Juristat 1994 homicide statistics, devoted an entire section to infant homicide, entitled "First Year of Life Holds Greatest Risk of Being Victim of Homicide."[11] Statistics Canada reports that 27 children under one year old were victims of homicide in 1994. This represents a significant increase over the previous 10 years' annual average of 20. Of these 27 babies who were killed last year, 20 were killed by parents.[12]

Of note is the fact that these data exclude many child abuse deaths. Child deaths caused by parents' criminal negligence and failure to provide the necessities of life, and starvation, both of which are criminal offenses, are not classified as homicides, and are not counted in these data. Statistics Canada states:

> In Canada, homicide is classified as first degree murder, second degree murder, manslaughter or infanticide. Deaths caused by criminal negligence, suicide, accidental or justifiable homicide are not included in the definition.[13]

In addition, many children's deaths by parental neglect are not counted in the 596 total. A *Globe and Mail* article of August 3, 1995, expressed this concern, reporting that:

> . . . the truth may be worse than the police statistics reveal. With the growing attention to child abuse has come a suspicion that some deaths previously categorized as accidental or unexplained may have been homicide.[14]

Statistics Canada reported that in 27 homicides of children under one year old, seven mothers were charged with infanticide.[15] Section 233 of the *Criminal Code* states that:

> A female person commits infanticide when by a wilful act or omission she causes the death of her newly-born child, if at the time of the act or omission she is not fully recovered from the effects of giving birth to the child and by reason thereof or to the effect of lactation consequent on the birth of the child her mind is disturbed.[16]

There is no medical relationship between lactation and murderous behaviour. The significant fact is the diminished responsibility and the slight sanctions granted women, even though some very brutal and premeditated murders are the result. Sometimes sanctions are as light as three months probation and suspended sentences.

In 1994, another report, *The Ontario Incidence for Reported Child Abuse and Neglect*, was released by the Toronto Institute of the Prevention of Child Abuse. It reviewed the 1993 child maltreatment investigations, 46,683[17] in total, by all 54 Children's Aid Societies of Ontario. Child maltreatment is defined by this study as any one of physical abuse, sexual abuse, child neglect, or child emotional maltreatment.[18] The findings were as follows: Of the total sustained cases of child maltreatment, mothers were perpetrators in 49 percent and fathers in 31 percent of the cases. In the category of child neglect, mothers were perpetrators in 85 percent of the substantiated cases. In the category of child physical abuse, biological mothers were perpetrators in 39 percent of the substantiated cases, and biological fathers in 40 percent of the cases. In the category of emotional maltreatment, mothers were perpetrators in 79 percent.[19] This study found that "boys were most strongly over-represented in the area of physical abuse, especially in the zero to three-year-old category, where boys accounted for 59 percent of the investigations."[20] Male children aged four to eleven years accounted for 55.5 percent.[21] The single largest category of investigated families, 35 percent, was the single mother family.[22] These data clearly reveal the imbalance in the current debate, showing that feminine aggression is most evident in child abuse. I shall now discuss feminine aggression in spousal violence.

Dr. Murray Straus and other scholars inform us that general population research examining domestic violence reveals that there is no statistical difference in the rates of violence perpetrated by men and women against each other and against their children. Recently, in a speech in Toronto on June 9, 1995 called *Corporal Punishment by Parents: Violence by Wives and Mothers*, Dr. Straus explained that "women hit just as often, and start it just as often as men do." Dr. Straus reveals the same in his article entitled "Physical Assaults By Wives: A Major Social Problem," saying that:

> Of the 495 couples in the 1985 National Family Violence Survey for whom one or more assaultive incidents were reported by a woman

respondent, the husband was the only violent partner in 25.9% of the cases, the wife was the only one to be violent in 25.5% of the cases, and both were violent in 48.6% of the cases.[23]

In Toronto, Dr. Straus gave data that the rate of husbands' violence has declined but wives' violence is unchanged.

The male of the species has received little concern in recent times. The evidence is that the male of the species has a difficult time even surviving. Let us review the state of survival of males. I just mentioned that 59 percent of the investigations of child abuse are of male children aged 0-3 years old. Male children are the recipients of most physical abuse. Dr. Eleanor Maccaby tells us that this is so even in lower primates, such as monkeys. She says that "We should be aware, however, that even among monkey mothers, a certain amount of differential socialization takes place. For example, they administer more punishment to male than female young, just as human parents do."[24] We also know that as Dr. Maccaby says, "parents more often enter into mutually coercive cycles of interaction with their sons."[25] We know that male children of single mothers are more likely to display aggression. We know that domestic discord affects male children adversely, and that behavioral and anti-social problems in male children are products of this domestic discord. We all know that the ratio of men to women detainees in our federal penitentiaries is 50:1; that is, 14,500 to 300. We know that male juvenile delinquency follows the same patterns. We know that more men die violently than women, and that the average life span of men is shorter than that of women. We also know that more men commit suicide than women. We further know that more men die in battle, in active combat and in the threats of war, than women. Morbidity rates, average life expectancy and the difficulties of being born inform us that male survival is truly miraculous. Dr. Eleanor Maccaby tells us that male fetuses are more vulnerable to the mishaps of pregnancy and childbirth, saying:

> ... A higher proportion of males than females are spontaneously aborted; the approximately equal sex ratio at birth exists only because more males than females are conceived. The incidence of various congenital defects is greater among male infants, ... greater male vulnerability remains, in fact, a puzzling one.[26]

The 1984 Vital Statistics published by the Register General of Ontario reveals that newly born male infants are more vulnerable in the post neo-natal period, accounting for 58 percent of deaths of infants aged 0-12 months. The 1984 statistics inform us that of 394 deaths of infants under 28 days, 230 were males.[27]

Violence in the family and brokenness state that as the child is raised, so shall the child be an adult; that the quality of parenting is the quality of future human beings. In 1976, A. Maurer reported in his paper "The Physical Punishment of Children" that his survey of violent offenders found that 100 percent of violent inmates in San Quentin prison had experienced violence between the ages of one to ten years.[28]

In 1973, A. Button reported in an article, "Some Antecedents of Felonious and Delinquent Behaviour," that these individuals had experienced violent upbringing, often at the hands of mothers.[29]

Child abuse and neglect are far too common. Daily, one observes yelling, screaming, scolding, hitting, slapping, kicking and yanking acted out by parents, usually mothers, in public places. Many think that this behavior is both normal and acceptable, that it is merely discipline, or tough love, not at all like the stories in the news. But it is abuse, the consequences of which will remain with a child well into its adult years. Some scars will never heal. The physical and psychological damage done to children is profound. A newly emerged form of child abuse is that from parents involved in matrimonial and custodial disputes. Parents use their children as bargaining tools, manipulating them to their own advantage, and causing parental alienation of the other parent. About children's pain and suffering during divorce and custody disputes, Dr. Hazel McBride, a Toronto-area psychologist, said, the children are ". . . put up as a prize or used as a weapon."[30]

The unspeakable human tragedy of family violence, the brokenness of children and of all the family members, and the resulting brokenness in society will not cease until both men and women cease their violence. The body politic of this nation needs care and healing.

End Notes

1. Steinmetz, Suzanne and M. Straus, *Violence in the Family*, New York: Harper and Row, 1974, p. 178.

2. Tardieu, Ambroise, quoted in *The Assault on Truth: Freud's Suppression of the Seduction Theory*, Jeffrey Masson, New York, 1984, pp. 18-19 as cited by Peter Silverman, *Who Speaks for the Children?*, Toronto, Ontario: Stoddart Publishing, Co., Ltd. 1989, pp. 114-115.

3. Silverman, Peter. *Who Speaks for the Children?* Ontario: Musson Book Company. 1978, p. 13.

4. *Ibid*, p. 13.

5. *Ibid.*, p. 20.

6. *Ibid.*, p. 17.

7. "Matthew 'At Risk' from Day He Was Born, Lawyer Says," *Vancouver Sun*, December 20, 1994, p. B7.

8. Judge Thomas Gove, "How to Put Children First," Vancouver Sun, June 7, 1995, Opinion Page.

9. Greenland, Cyril. "Preventing Child Abuse and Neglect Deaths: The Identification and Management of High Risk Cases," *Health Visitor*, July 1986, vol. 59, p. 205.

10. *Ibid.*, p. 205.

11. Statistics Canada, *Homicide in Canada - 1994*, August 1995, *Juristat*, vol. 15., no. 11 catalogue no. 85-002, p. 14.

12. *Ibid.*, p. 14.

13. *Ibid.*, p. 2.

14. Henry Hess, "Babies in First Year Risk Murder Most," *Globe and Mail*, August 3, 1995, p. A5.

15. Statistics Canada, *op. cit.*, p. 14.

16. Criminal Code of Canada, RSC 1985, c. C-46 *Martin's Annual Criminal Code 1994*, Canada Law Book, Inc., Ontario, 1993, Section 233, p. 353.

17. Report of the Institute for the Prevention of Child Abuse, *Ontario Incidence Study of Reported Child Abuse and Neglect 1994*, p. iii.

18. *Ibid.*, p. I.

19. *Ibid.*, p. 67.

20. *Ibid.*, p. 82.

21. *Ibid.*, p. 85.

22. *Ibid.*, p. xii.

23. Gelles, Richard J. And Loseke, Donileen R., *Current Controversies on Family Violence*, CA: Sage Publications, 1993, p. 74.

24. Maccaby, Eleanor E., *Social Development: Psychological Growth and the Parent-Child Relationship*, New York: Harcourt Brace Jovanovich, Inc., 1980, p. 244.

25. *Ibid.*, p. 244.

26. *Ibid.*, p. 206.

27. Registrar General of Ontario, *Vital Statistics for 1984*, Province of Ontario, p. 68.

28. Gelles, Richard J., *Family Violence*, CA: Sage Publications, Inc., 1979., p. 68.

29. *Ibid.*, pp. 179, 180.

30. "The Way Courts Handle Custody Cases Needs Overhaul, Psychologist Warns," *The Montreal Gazette*, September 18, 1995, p. A3.

Welfare Reform: How Do Children Fare?

Carol Statuto Bevan
Professional Staff Member, U.S. House of Representatives,
Committee on Ways and Means

It has been fifteen years since P.L. 96-272, the Foster Care and Adoption Assistance Act, became law. This fifteen year experiment that combined the concept of reasonable efforts to keep families together with the notion of permanency planning for children has been a dismal failure. Despite the expenditure of billions of federal and state dollars, the number of children who do not experience either a rehabilitated family or a permanent family has grown. In fact, the percentage of children in foster care from between two and five years old has increased significantly since 1983.[1] The median length of stay in foster care for all age groups has increased,[2] while there has been a significant decrease in the number of adoptions of children out of foster care.[3]

It is the contention of this article that the trend to focus child welfare services on preserving families and averting foster care placement is wrong. This focus risks the safety and welfare of too many children. The paramount standard in child welfare must be preserving the child's welfare.

P.L. 96-272: Flawed Assumptions and Bad Results

It is time to ask the question: Is the policy stance of P.L. 96-272 something that we as a nation ought to continue to subsidize? Is it not time to look at the results of this Act and seriously question its direction? While no one can doubt that the intentions behind P.L. 96-272 are laudable, this article will show what the result has been. The foster care population has not declined.[4] The number of children who find permanent homes through adoption has fallen dramatically.[5] Death rates among very young children have hit a 40 year high, despite the entitlement of protective services through the use of foster care.[6] Babies are staying in the limbo of foster care longer than any other age group.[7] Children of color are waiting twice as long for adoptive homes, simply because of the color of their skin.[8] Young girls who have been sexually abused are not getting much-needed services in the system.[9] Two-thirds of the children in foster care are being returned to families that often still are not safe, resulting in a re-entry into foster care with a re-entry rate as high as 33%.[10] The length of time that children spend in foster care has increased significantly with some children remaining, on average, four to six years without permanent homes.[11]

Good intentions aside, it is clear that the safety and long term protection of children cannot be assured in the current system.

P.L. 96-272 is based on two flawed assumptions: (one) that the foster care system can balance the safety needs of children with preserving the family; and, (two) that if one creates a system that is financed and perpetuated by the number of children in the system, that permanency can somehow be achieved.

The assumption behind P.L. 96-272 that keeps children in foster care for years while exhaustive efforts are made to "fix" the family rests on the erroneous belief that children always do better remaining or being reunited with their biological families and that adoption as an intervention should always be a last resort. However, when one examines the data, it is clear that these policies are misguided.

A second assumption behind P.L. 96-272 is that by making every at-risk child theoretically "entitled" to foster care, which by its very design is a temporary placement, that permanency can somehow be achieved. The fact is that most of the federal spending for child welfare is spent on the "room and board" or maintenance of low-income children in foster care. Foster Care (IV-E) is an open-ended entitlement that costs billions. Yet, there is little evidence that spending billions on foster care payments has promoted child well-being through achieving permanency for the thousands of children in foster care.

Family Preservation Does Not Work

The fascination with family preservation services ignores several realities. It does not work.[12] Since it is difficult to identify the specific type of family which can benefit from rehabilitation services and which family will kill the child despite services, family preservation services must be targeted to a highly select group of families or society will risk the child's life.[13] Not all family forms are equally effective in nurturing and raising healthy, productive children, which leads to a very important question that needs to be raised and that is not being raised. That question is: To what extent is a mother who has exposed several children to drugs in utero, and who has had these children already removed from her custody because of abuse, a "family" that ought to be "preserved"? It is time to shift the focus from family preservation to child preservation. It is time to measure the success of child welfare services on how well these services promote the welfare of children.

New Paradigm: A Child Centered Model

In developing a child focused, child centered foster care and adoption system, the overriding principle must be that child preservation not family preservation, or family reunification, must be the outcome and the standard used to measure the success of any intervention.

A child centered model would embody principles that are sensitive to children's development that children's needs are different at different developmental stages that are often, but not always, age related.

- A child centered restructuring of foster care would include financial assistance to states (through demonstration grants or other means) to expedite legal proceedings to reduce the delays experienced by children with adoption plans.
- A child centered paradigm would base the timing of the dispositional hearing and the evaluation of the case plan on the child's sense of time and developmental needs.
- Child centered policies would take the harm that happens to children through abuse and neglect seriously.
- A child centered model would respect the attachments that children form.
- A child centered system would reject any "one size fits all fix" and focus on assessments based on the needs of a particular child, in a particular circumstance, with a particular history.
- A child centered policy would give adoption parity with other child welfare services such as family reunification, family preservation, long-term foster care and kinship care.
- A child centered paradigm would establish citizen review panels made up of local citizens who are neither on county nor state payroll.
- A child centered model would promote research and the collection of nationwide data on how children are faring in the child welfare system.

A child centered model would recognize adoption as a legitimate, family-building activity that should be supported though our public laws (subsidies, tax credits), the judicial system (expedited adoption tracks, child welfare cases given priority, best interests of the child standard), private corporations (employee benefits, insurance coverage), religious organizations (maternity home services, counseling, adoption services), and the intellectual community (research that fairly reflects the positive outcomes for children, birthmothers, and adoptive families must be conducted and published).

This article raises more questions than it answers. The President has vetoed welfare reform that would have block-granted much of foster care. Currently there is a new proposal by the National Governors Association that would retain foster care and adoption assistance as well as the Independent Living Programs as entitlements. There is very little anyone can say with certainty about the effect of current welfare reform efforts, except that the focus is not on the child. Very little attention is being paid to the child welfare system by anyone except the House of

Representative Republicans. For the Senate and the President as well as the Governors, it is child welfare as usual, and that means doing "too much, too little, too early, too late."

The child welfare system is expected to do "too much" in the sense that there are those both inside and outside the system who operate under the assumption that all families can be turned around and made "good enough" parents with the provision of supportive family services. These services -- from parent counseling, child care, and enrollment in drug rehabilitation programs to in-home "family preservation programs" -- are in many cases insufficient to change the behavior of the family to the extent that the child can remain safely in the home. This is not to argue that these services not be provided, but rather to contend that not all families are equally good candidates for particular types of intervention. For example, in-home family preservation services are not likely to benefit those families that have long histories of drug involvement and/or have had several children placed in foster care for significant periods, or have serious re-abuse records in their backgrounds.[14] For some families, what would work to successfully turn these families around has not yet been discovered. Under these circumstances, it is asking "too much" for this type of family to be able to overcome its dysfunction to the extent that the child can safely be returned home or avoid placement in foster care, given what is currently known about treatment intervention strategies, success rates of various modalities and this particular family's history.

Success rates for rehabilitation programs are generally low. There do not yet exist the kinds of assessment tools that can predict which families would be good candidates for particular modalities of intervention.[15] Not a lot is known about how to change the kinds of "hard core" families that are increasingly entering the child welfare system, and without this knowledge the child welfare system is expected to do "too much."

The child welfare system does "too little" in the sense that what is known is not put into practice. For example, it is a basic child development principle that what infants and young children need most in their lives is stability, continuity and the chance to have someone who is "crazy" about them. Yet it is infants and young children who spend the longest amounts of time in the temporary families that foster care provides. It should not be a surprise that despite the tragically low rate of adoption out of foster care (less than eight percent), the families who adopt these children are most often the ones who have had the opportunity to "fall in love" with them -- the foster parents. Here again the system does "too little" to facilitate the provision of a "forever" family to a child in need of one.

Another example of where the system does "too little" is in the timing, targeting and provision of family support interventions. There is considerable evidence over decades from Yale University that shows that high quality family support services provided by a team of professionals (including psychologists, clinical social workers, physicians and nurses) to troubled and impoverished new parents can make a long term difference in terms of better outcomes for children as well as increased functioning for the families.[16] Limiting some kinds of interventions until a child gets hurt is not a policy based on research and indeed does "too little."

"Too early" refers to two different phenomena: First, "about one in three children entering foster care today has been in care previously."[17] This can be interpreted as meaning that the children were returned "too early" and were subsequently put again at risk. The assumption that the family was "fixed" was made "too early," and with dire consequences for the child. Another meaning of the characterization "too early" refers to the increasing number of cases that are reported as child abuse, but upon investigation the report is deemed "unsubstantiated," meaning abuse "was not indicated." According to Douglas Besharov (who was the first director of the U.S. National Center on Child Abuse and Neglect), the rise in "unsubstantiated" child abuse cases accompanied by a rise in foster care caseloads signals a misuse of the foster care system and a misdiagnosis of the policy problem as abuse when in fact it is poverty.[18] The assumption by many parents is that the state intervenes "too early" into the lives of families, and that in so doing the power of the state is being misused and clogging the child welfare system.

The "too late" reference refers to the increasing length of time that too many children spend in foster care. For example, a recent newspaper item[19] documented the case of a newborn boy abandoned on a "frigid curb" in Maryland. When questioned about the fate of this child the Social Service Department spokeswoman "would only say that her agency generally tries to find a way to return infants to their parents, a process that can take anywhere from six months to three years." To allow a newborn to spend as long as three years until the Social Services Department makes a permanent plan for the child is "too late." According to a 1995 General Accounting Office Report, "infants are staying in foster care longer than any other age group."[20] The wait for a child in foster care for whom adoption is planned is on average four to six years, according to the same report. The first three years of a child's life are critical to the child's subsequent growth and development, including the child's ability to trust, to love and to ultimately be loved. This chapter is policy driven because changes need to be made in the child welfare system -- specifically P.L. 96-272, the Adoption Assistance and Child Welfare Act of 1980, and the Child Abuse Prevention and Treatment Act, as well as state laws that act as barriers to finding permanent families for children. Where research is useful it is cited. Where state or federal innovations are observed or promised they will be noted. If there is a bias in the writing of this report it stems from the author's belief that there are many parts of the child welfare system that don't work -- from structure and financial incentives to ideology and practice -- but it is time to recognize that children can not be held hostage while the system is being repaired. The author shares a sense of urgency with many others in the field in seeing to it that changes are made in the system but, unlike others, stresses that all the parts of the system cannot be perfected while children wait.

Childhood does not wait. If a bias exists in the selection of a particular research finding or in a policy advocated, it is that for too long the child welfare system has been unable to develop a standard that says we have erred in pondering the causes of family dysfunction, researching intervention strategies, and devising administrative and legal remedies, all while the children are kept waiting. Given the author's bias to keep front and center the needs of children at different developmental ages, this does not mean that the author is against research on either the macro or micro level or the provision of services to families in need. Clearly, what these children need most are families. The author's bias is taking seriously the harm that children experience, who are without stable and loving families, and making this harm the standard against which the effectiveness of a policy, the successfulness of an intervention or the usefulness of a research study is judged.

Family Preservation: What Is Being Preserved?

Models of intervention strategies to preserve the family are intended to avert the threatened foster care placement and reduce the risk of further harm to the child and family by the provision of an intensive basket of short term services lasting, on average, about six weeks. One of the most cherished assumptions of the family preservation movement is that most, if not all, families can be turned around well enough to parent their children in non-abusive ways.[21]

The largest randomized experiment on family preservation programs involved the Families First program in Illinois. The major findings of this study, conducted by Chapin Hall/University of Chicago researchers, was that the provision of these "services does not appear to have had a significant effect on the likelihood of further harm to children or placement in substitute care."[22] Furthermore, the authors write, "Our approach here must recognize that there is little evidence that many of the programs currently being tried have more than minimal effects."[23] The findings of the largest randomized experiment conducted so far on a family preservation program found that it did not work. "We found little effect of the Families First program on placement, subsequent maltreatment, and rate of case closing, and we have found that effects on family functioning are probably relatively limited."[24]

This finding is consistent with the findings of the U.S. Advisory Board on Child Abuse and Neglect: "The minimal research conducted in this area has not identified specific behaviors that can single out parents whose action or inaction might end a child's life."[25] Without the identification of specific behaviors that can single out parents whose action or inaction might end a child's life, the provision of intensive services to keep families together will put some children in harm's way.

The family preservation movement represents, in part, the view that the rights of the biological parents should be paramount over any right the child might claim.

of the biological parents should be paramount over any right the child might claim. Despite what is known about the limitations of family preservation services, family preservation ideology prevails. It prevails because it is consistent with several prevailing ideologies, especially one that says more government and more money will ease this social problem. It prevails because in 1993 Congress allocated one billion dollars to improve the foster care system with half the money going to family preservation services. Clearly, money drives the child welfare system and determines, in part, the policy solutions. What this means for foster care is that family preservation services have become the option of choice.

The impact of family preservation ideology hits the fastest growing age group entering foster care the hardest -- babies and preschoolers. This age group is not only more likely to enter care, but once in care tends to experience longer stays.[26] The median length of stay in foster care for all children increased in the nineties but, incredibly, infants endured the longest spells of out-of-home care. Goerge, Wulczyn and Harden observed that "in California, Michigan, and New York, children who enter foster care as infants are remaining in care longer than those in any other entry age group. For New York, the median duration for infants is over 42 months, more than one year longer than for any other children."[27]

By ignoring these specific realities it is clear that the current trend in child welfare assumes incorrectly that every individual who conceives a child is a competent parent; that the provision of government services can correct any shortcoming; and that the preservation of the biological family is the ultimate social service goal. If this were not the case, family preservation and family reunification would not be the overwhelming focus of intervention in child welfare, and the focus would be centered on the child. How else can one explain the fact that adoption and even foster care have been demonized while family preservation and family reunification efforts have been elevated?

The author is not arguing against a family model, but against the dichotomy that it sets up: either (biological) family or children. It seems that to uniformly elevate this model above all others, without the research that shows the model works to promote the safety of children and the strengthening of the family, is a tragic mistake. A mistake that will be heavily funded over the next five years is indeed tragic. Clearly, a paradigm that promotes in-home family preservation services for all children will put many children at risk of re-abuse. The University of Chicago researchers know it and in fact have said it, as reported by Patrick Murphy in his Congressional testimony: "Chapin Hall (University of Chicago) pointed out that it is almost certain that the probability of child deaths would be higher in a program in which children at risk are left at home rather than to be taken into foster care."[28] Why are these data not driving child welfare policy?

Family Reunification, Foster Care Placement, Adoption: How Children Fare

An examination of the different placement options (family reunification, foster care, and adoption) shows that the developmental outcome for children is least favorable when the child is returned home.[29] The developmental outcomes for children returned home showed worse physical care, lower school attendance, inferior achievement scores, lower adjustment measures, and lower IQ ratings.

In a study by Fanshel and Shinn, children who were returned home failed to test as high on IQ scales as those who remained in foster care over a five year period.[30] These findings have important implications when one considers that children are being returned home after shorter stays only to return again to foster care placement. This is not to argue for longer stays in foster care, but that policy makers should consider that for some children a longer stay could provide more stability than a round trip home and then back again.

In Michael Wald's study comparing children given services in foster care with children given services at home, those served at home received worse physical care, had lower school attendance and inferior achievement scores.[31] The findings of this study led Wald and his Stanford colleagues to conclude: "Unless interventions significantly improve parental functioning, children left at home remain at substantial risk."[32]

The belief that foster care is bad for children is central to both the family reunification and family preservation paradigms. In the words of the University of Chicago researchers: "As family preservation programs have expanded, foster care has become demonized."[33] It is time to put this notion to rest by examining the research on the effects of foster care on children.

In a review and synthesis of twenty-seven foster care studies conducted over the past thirty years, McDonald, *et. al.* wrote: "Contrary to current thinking, children in foster care for longer times do better than those returned to their biological homes after a short time."[34]

Festinger found no differences between the outcomes for her now-adult foster care graduates in New York City and the general population on most characteristics, including arrests, self-esteem and happiness.[35] Jones and Moses, in a large study of former foster care children in West Virginia, found that young adults who age out of foster care after an average of five years in the system have rates of marriage, broken marriages, incarceration, parenthood and marital satisfaction that are comparable to the general population.[36]

A study of foster care children who had been in care at least one year and on average five years found, not surprisingly, that those children were reported by social workers to be more attached to their foster homes than to their birth homes.[37]

The point here is that, clearly, foster care can be a good alternative for children who are at risk by either remaining with or returning to their biological families. While conclusions should be cautiously drawn from these studies on foster care outcomes, it seems evident that policies based on the belief that foster care is always bad for children, particularly when compared to leaving them in the home or reuniting them with maladaptive parents, have little basis in research.[38]

In the classic work by Goldstein, Freud and Solnit entitled "Beyond the Best Interests of the Child," the case is made that children form the ties that bind by falling in love with their day-to-day caretakers. Young children are blissfully unaware of blood ties (until later in their development) but are very much aware of those who love them, feed them, comfort them, etc.[39] It is the psychological family that needs to be preserved to prevent further harm to the child. It is the creation of attachment bonds, where there are none, that will make a real difference in the child's life. The adoption process can establish attachment bonds where there were none and can create a psychological family.

The success of adoption rests, of course, on the subsequent adjustment of the child. This adjustment is dependent, in part, on the child's prior history (of abuse, neglect and number of foster care placements), as well as the child's age at adoption. The research on children adopted out of foster care is sparse but it shows that adjustment for many of these children is not traumatic.

The majority of adopted children adjust successfully.[40] On measures of identity and self-esteem, adopted adolescents rate themselves favorably.[41] In a study of mental health problems, Triseliotis and Russell found no differences between older adoptees and the general population. Children adopted transracially show no differences in terms of identity formation and self-esteem, attachment to parents, or psychological health.[42] Finally, the fact that adoptive parents can and do fulfill children's developmental needs, provide home environments conducive to child rearing, and that adopted children fare well was borne out by a study conducted by Nicholas Zill of Westat Corporation.[43]

In 1994, The Search Institute released the findings of the largest study ever of adoptive families in the United States. This four year survey studied 715 families who adopted infants through private agencies between 1974 and 1980. A total of 881 adopted adolescents, 1,262 parents and 78 non-adopted siblings participated. The findings reveal that :

> . . . on a series of measures about the formation of identity, we find little evidence that adopted adolescents are particularly vulnerable. When asked to compare themselves to others their age, adopted adolescents report satisfactory resolution of identity concerns at rates as high or higher than their peers. And on an index of self-esteem, adopted adolescents compare favorably to a national sample of 12-18 year olds. This finding runs counter to the classical understanding of adopted adolescents. Why the discrepancy? The classical view is based to a considerable extent on clinical samples and a wider spectrum of adoptions, including those that occur after infancy.[44]

This study has compelling implications for child welfare policy, especially as it relates to the increased numbers of infants found in the child welfare system. The study did find a relationship between age of placement and strength of attachment: the earlier the placement, the stronger the attachment. This is not to say that attachment for older placements was not strong because, in fact, overall attachment rates were high. But as a matter of public policy, the data are quite clear that expedited placements of children into permanent settings where attachments can form have better outcomes for children. A closer examination of The Search Institute's findings show how the adoption option can meet the standard of promoting the best interests of the child and protecting the child from harm.

- Adoptive children are less likely to live with a single parent.
- Adoptive parents are more likely to have college degrees.
- The adoptive families in the study exhibit considerable strength in family dynamics
- Adopted adolescents show no differences in self-rating of mental illness or self-esteem.
- Children adopted transracially showed no differences in terms of identity formation and self esteem, attachment to parents, or psychological health.

This last finding is consistent with the findings of Simon (1977) and Simon and Altstein (1987). A landmark study that is consistent with the findings from The Search Institute, in terms of showing that adoptive parents can and do fulfill children's developmental needs, that the home environments provided by adoptive parents are very conducive to child rearing, and that adopted children fare well, was conducted by Nicholas Zill of Westat Corporation.[45] The data presented in the Congressional testimony were drawn from several sources: "The data . . . are drawn from a large federal survey conducted by the National Center for Health Statistics of the U.S. Department of Health and Human Services . . . the information . . . goes beyond the published report to include additional analyses on measures of children's academic performance. It also includes results from an earlier study using data on adopted and other children from the 1981 National Health Interview Survey on Child Health."[46] Zill compared adopted children living in families with: "(1) children born to unmarried mothers who are being raised by those mothers in single parent families; (2) children who live with one or two grandparents, but apart from both of their birth parents; and (3) children who live with both of their birth parents."[47]

Zill compared the social and economic circumstances of the four groups and found that "adopted children are actually privileged . . . (A)doptive parents tend to be well above average in terms of education, income, family stability and other characteristics that social scientists have found to correlate with favorable outcomes for children."[48] Zill notes that "(L)ess than one percent of adopted children received Aid to Families with Dependent Children, whereas among white children born outside of marriage and raised by their biological mothers, 32% were receiving welfare."[49]

The quality of home environments was measured by looking at regular bedtimes, the use of seatbelts, and other measures. Overall, the home environments provided to adopted children were above average on each of these indicators.

Access to medical care was measured by health insurance coverage, dental visits and a family pediatrician. The access to medical care provided to adopted children was better than all three of the comparison populations. In fact, Zill commented that "it appears that adoptive parents tend to be especially scrupulous about obtaining preventive care for their children and getting professional attention for any problem or potential problem, whether it be medical, educational, or developmental."[50]

Health status was measured by parental ratings of their children's health, the "mean number of days children in the group spent in bed during the last year due to illness or injury; the mean number of physician contacts they had during the last year; and the number of hospital visits during the last year."[51] Adopted children were reported to be in excellent health (56%), essentially the same proportion as children living with both parents (55%). "By contrast, only a minority of children living with unmarried mothers (41%) and children living with grandparents (39%) were reported to be in optimal health."[52]

"Adopted children had about the same average number of days in bed per year due to illness or injury (3.8) as children living with both biological parents (3.9)."[53] By contrast, adopted children had one more physician contact per year (5.4), on average, than children living with unmarried mothers (4.5), and nearly one more than children living with both biological parents (4.7). This probably reflects the greater access to medical care that adopted children have and the readiness of adoptive parents to seek care.[54] Adoptive children had, by a significant margin, the "lowest rate of hospital use," leading Zill to conclude that "while adoptive families have good access to care and a propensity to contact physicians at a higher-than-average rate, their use of medical care seems appropriate and relatively cost-effective."[55]

One interesting finding concerned one measure of academic performance, the number of children reported by their parents as having been suspended from school. Adopted children and children living with both birth parents, aged 7-17 years, had relatively low suspension scores (6% and 5%, respectively), contrasted with 17% among children living with unmarried mothers. We would interpret these findings to indicate that the two parent families exerted considerably more control over their children than the single parent families and that this could and probably would influence the life course that these children pursued. If suspension is related to dropping out of school and low academic performance, and if these variables are, in turn, related to poor job prospects as well as marriage prospects, then this finding should cause some alarm among policy makers.

To measure the prevalence of psychological disorders, parents were asked to report on the presence of "delays in growth or development, learning disabilities, and emotional or behavioral problems that lasted three or more months or required psychological treatment."[56] The majority of adopted children were reported by their parents not to have a delay in growth or development, a learning disability, or emotional or behavioral problems that required psychological treatment. However, 36% of the adopted children were reported to have one of these problems, compared to only 15% for children living with both birth parents. Children living with unmarried mothers and those living with a grandparent received scores that were in-between the scores for the adopted children and those living with both parents.

In interpreting these findings, Zill cautioned that this measure called upon the parents to report on the prevalence of these disorders, and that differential underreporting could be attributed to such factors as an unfamiliarity with the terms involved, an unwillingness to seek mental health services, or a lack of access to health care professionals who would identify psychological disorders on the part of the lower-educated parents as compared to the higher-educated adopted parents, who are more likely to be familiar with the clinical terms. "Possible reasons for the higher prevalence of psychological disorders among adopted children include genetic explanations, explanations that emphasize the willingness of adopted parents to obtain psychological help for problems that might not receive clinical attention from other families . . ."[57] We might also add that adoptive parents receive detailed medical background information as a part of the adoption process -- biological parents may not have amassed such information.

Within a finding that underscores the importance of expedited placement of infants into adoptive homes, is the finding that differences were found between those children placed into adoptive homes in infancy and those placed after infancy in the reported patterns of seeking and obtaining psychological treatment. "Among adolescents who had been adopted during the first year of life, 13% had seen a psychologist or psychiatrist at some point. Among adolescents adopted after infancy, however, the comparable figure was 42%."[58] These data indicate that the risk that adopted children face is not the adoption *per se*; it is in the wait to be adopted. The challenge to policy makers is to reduce the risk to children not from the experience of adoption, but from the experience of abuse and re-abuse, and the multiple placements often associated with the child welfare system.

When comparing the "adoption option" to long-term foster care or residential care, the outcomes for children in adoption are the more compelling, especially in light of its place in the child welfare services hierarchy. Children placed in adoptive homes scored better on measures of family adjustment and emotional and developmental functioning than either children returned home or those in long-term foster care.[59] In a study that compared educational attainment in adoptive, foster and residential placements, adopted children had superior educational attainment. It is important to note that in this sample 62% of the adopted children were under the age of three years when placed.[60]

After reviewing these studies, a picture of adoption emerges that shows the psychological, physical and educational benefits to children of adoption. This picture should lead policy makers concerned about child welfare reform to the conclusion that adoption should at least emerge as a competing alternative to the family reunification, family preservation, and long-term foster care models for more children, in increasingly more circumstances. It is important to underscore that this is not to argue for policies that would reduce treatment services to families in need, nor is this to argue for public policies that are more coercive, intrusive or punitive. It is to state that adoption as a matter of public policy does benefit children, and ought not be overlooked in the welfare reform debate.

Adoption services, including the termination of parental rights, ought to be as aggressively and enthusiastically pursued as family maintenance and family reunification services are, but clearly this is not the case. Given the fact that half of the children who come into care are maltreated, does it surprise anyone that two-thirds of these children are returned to these same families and there is an estimated re-entry rate back into the system as high as 33%? Does anyone really believe that 66% of the maltreating families change sufficiently to put them in charge of nurturing and protecting their children? The fact that only 7% of the children are adopted out of foster care speaks volumes about how adoption is viewed by the child welfare system.

Devolution alone is insufficient to bring about the radical reform that is necessary to protect children in our country. However, devolution that fully embraces a child-centered paradigm will take more children out of harm's way. The federal government ought to condition federal money going to the states for child welfare on the state's adherence to child-centered principles. States must get the bold message that they must be accountable for how they do child welfare and that they must do child welfare differently. Child-centered principles that allow the flexibility to "let a thousand flowers bloom" while at the same time promote children's safety and developmental needs as the paramount standards against which any experimentation is deemed successful must be part of any worthwhile welfare reform package.

End Notes

1.Tatara, T. (1993a) *Characteristics of Children in Substitute and Adoptive Care: A Statistical Summary of the VCIS National Child Welfare Data Base.* Washington, D.C.: American Public Welfare Association.

2. *Ibid.*

3. *Ibid.*

4. Tatara, T. (1995) U.S. Child Substitute Care Flow Data for FY 93 and Trends in the State Child Substitute Care Populations. *VCIS Research Notes,* (11).

5. Tatara (1993a) *op. cit.*

6. U.S. Advisory Board on Child Abuse and Neglect. (1995) *A Nation's Shame: Fatal Child Abuse and Neglect in the United States.* U.S. Department of Health and Human Services, Administration for Children and Families, Fifth Report.

7. Goerge, R.M., Wulcyzn, F. & Harden, A.W., (1994a) *An Update from the Multi-State Foster Care Data Archive: Foster Care Dynamics 1983-1993.* Chicago: Chapin Hall Center for Children, University of Chicago; Tatara, T. (1993a) *op. cit.*; U.S. Department of Health and Human Services. (1993) *Report to Congress: National Abandoned Infants.* U.S. Department of Health and Human Services.; Barth, R. "The Reunification of Very Young Children From Foster Care," *The Source*, 15(1), 1995.

8. Barth, R., Courtney, M. and Needell, B. (1994) "The Odds of Adoption vs. Remaining in Long-Term Foster Care." Paper Presented at the Second Annual Child Welfare Conference Washington, D.C.; Tatara, T. "A Comparison of Child Substitute Care Exit Rates Among Three Different Racial/Ethnic Groups in 12 States, FY 84 to FY 90." *VCIS Research Notes*, (9), 1994.

9. Mech, E.V., Leonard, E.L., & Pryde, J.A. (1994) "Female Victims of Childhood Sexual Abuse Who Are Placed In Foster Care: Treatment and Program Issues." Paper presented at National Council For Adoption Conference on Foster Care, Boys Town, Nebraska, May 20-22.

10. Barth, R.P., Needell, B., Berrick, J.D., Albert, V. & Jonson-Reid, M. (1995) "Child Welfare Services To Young Children." Paper presented at the Third Annual National Child Welfare Conference, Washington, D.C.; Goerge, R.M. (1990) "The Reunification Process in Substitute Care." *Social Service Review*, 64, (3), 422-457.; Tatara, T. (1993a), *op. cit.*

11. Kusserow, R. (1991) *Barriers to Freeing Children For Adoption.* Washington, D.C.: U.S. Department of Health and Human Services. Office of the Inspector General; Tatara, T. (1993a), *op. cit.*

12. Schuerman, J.R., Rzepnicki, T.L., & Littel, J.H. (1994) *Putting Families First: An Experiment in Family Preservation.* New York: Aldine De Gruyter.

13. U.S. Advisory Board on Child Abuse and Neglect. (1995) *A Nation's Shame: Fatal Child Abuse and Neglect in the United States.* U.S. Department of Health and Human Services, Administration for Children and Families, Fifth Report.

14. Howard, J. (1994) "Barriers to Successful Intervention." In D.J. Besharov, ed. *When Drug Addicts Have Children.* Washington, D.C.: Child Welfare League of America and American Enterprise Institute, pp. 91-100.

15. Condon, C.M. (1995) Clinton's Cocaine Babies. *Policy Review,* Spring, 1995; Howard, J. (1994), *op. cit.*

16. Seitz, V., Rosenbaum, L.K., & Apfel, N.H. (1985) "Effects of Family Support Intervention: A Ten-Year Follow-up." *Child Development,* 56:376-391.

17. National Center For Children In Poverty. (1991) *Child Welfare Reform.* Report Series, October. New York: School of Public Health, Columbia University.

18. Besharov, D.J. (1986) "The Misuse of Foster Care: When the Desire to Help Children Outruns the Ability to Improve Parental Functioning." *Family Law Quarterly,* XX,(1); Besharov, D.J. (1994) "Don't Call It Child Abuse If It's Really Poverty." Paper presented at the Social Policies For Children Conference held at Woodrow Wilson School of Public and International Affairs, Princeton, N.J.

19. *The Washington Times,* December 27, 1995.

20. U.S. General Accounting Office. (1995) *Child Welfare: Complex Needs Strain Capacity To Provide Services.* (GAO/HEH-95-208 Foster Care Review, September 1995). Washington, D.C.

21. Rossi, P. (1990) *Evaluating Family Preservation Services: A Report to the Edna McConnell Clark Foundation.* Mass.: University of Mass.

22. Schuerman, J.R., Rzepnicki, T.L., & Littel, J.H. (1994) *op. cit.*

23. *Ibid.*

24. *Ibid.*

25. U.S. Advisory Board on Child Abuse and Neglect (1995) *op. cit.*

26. Goerge, R.M., Wulcyzn, F. & Harden, A.W. (1994a) *op. cit.*

27. Goerge, R.M., Wulcyzn, F. & Harden, A.W. (1994b) *op. cit.*

28. Murphy, J. (1994) "Please Don't Send Me Home!" Paper presented at the National Council for Adoption Conference on Foster Care, Boys Town, Nebraska, May 20-22.

29. Barth, R.P., & Berry, M. (1987) "Outcomes of Child Welfare Services Under Permanency Planning." *Social Service Review,* 61; Lahti, J. (1978) *A Follow-Up Study of the Oregon Project.* Portland, Ore.: Regional Research Institute for Human Services, Portland State University; McDonald, T., Allen, R., Westerfelt, A. & Piliavin, I. (1992) "What We Know About the Effects of Foster Care. *Focus,* 14(2); Wald, M. (1994) "Termination of Parental Rights." In D.J. Besharov (ed.), *When Drug Addicts Have Children,* pp.195-210. Washington, D.C.: Child Welfare League of American and American Enterprise Institute.

30. Fanshel, D. (1978) *Children in Foster Care: A Longitudinal Investigation.* New York: Columbia University Press.

31. Wald, M. (1994), *op. cit.*

32. *Ibid.*

33. Schuerman, J.R., Rzepnicki, T.L., & Littel, J.H. (1994), *op. cit.*

34. McDonald, T., Allen, R., Westerfelt, A. & Piliavin, I. (1992), *op. cit.*

35. Festinger, T. (1983) *No One Ever Asked Us: A Postscript to Foster Care.* New York: Columbia University Press.

36. Jones, M.A. & Moses, B. (1984) *West Virginia's Former Foster Children: Their Experiences In Care and Their Lives As Young Adults.* New York: Child Welfare League of America.

37. Fanshel, D. (1982) "Foster Care As a Two Tiered System." *Children and Youth Services Review,* 14.

38. *Ibid.*; Festinger, T. (1983), *op. cit.*; Jones, M.A. & Moses, B. (1984), *op. cit.*; McDonald, T., Allen, R., Westerfelt, A. & Piliavin, I. (1992), *op. cit.*

39. Goldstein, J., Freud, A. & Solnit, A.J. (1973) *Beyond The Best Interests Of the Child.* New York: The Free Press.

40. Brodzinsky, D.M., & Schecter, M.D. (eds), (1990) *The Psychology of Adoption.* New York: Oxford University Press.

41. Benson, P., Sharma, A.R. & Roehlkepartain, E.C. (1994). *Growing Up Adopted: A Portrait of Adolescents & Their Families.* Minneapolis, Minn.: Search Institute.

42. Simon, R. and Altstein, H. (1977) *Transracial Adoption.* New York: Wiley, 1977; Simon, R., & Altstein, H. (1987) *Transracial Adoptees and Their Families: A Study of Identity and Commitment.* New York: Praeger, 1987.

43. Zill, N. (1995) "Adopted Children in the United States: A Profile Based on a National Survey of Child Health." Congressional Testimony. Committee on Ways and Means, U.S. House of Representatives, May 10.

44. Benson, P., Sharma, A.R. & Roehlkepartain, E.C. (1994), *op. cit.*

45. Zill, N. (1995), *op. cit.*

46. - 58. *Ibid.*

59. Lahti, J. (1978), *op. cit.*

60. Triseliotis, J. & Russell, J. (1984) *Hard to Place: The Outcome of Adoption and Residential Care.* London: Heinemann.

Separate is Not Equal: Challenging State-Sponsored Barriers to Interracial Adoptions

Donna Matias, Staff Attorney
Institute for Justice, Washington, D.C.

*So I can dream of a day, perhaps nearer than I think, when childless parents
will take a child for their own without caring what the color of the skin may be.
On that day prejudice will really be ended and the ultimate reach of love
achieved.*[1]

I. Matthew's and Joseph's story

I'd like to start out with the story of Matthew O. and Joseph I., African
American brothers the Institute for Justice represents in its interracial adoption
lawsuit in Texas. On my first day on the job at the Institute for Justice, a woman
named Lou Ann Mullen called me from Lexington, Texas. Lou Ann had been
Matthew's foster mother and had been trying to adopt him and his brother;
however, state social workers had other plans for the boys. I begin with Matthew
and Joseph because, as I've learned since my first conversation with Lou Ann, their
story is all too common among minority children nationwide who await loving,
permanent homes.

Matthew was born with syphilis, crack-addicted, and suffering a liver disorder
as a result of his young mother's constant drug and alcohol abuse. He was the fifth
of eight children, almost all of whom were born with disorders relating to substance
abuse, and all of whom -- except for the two sets of twins -- had different fathers.
By the time he came into the world, the Texas Department of Protective and
Regulatory Services (DPRS) had all of Matthew's siblings in its custody. Matthew
was born a ward of the state.

At nine days old, Matthew was placed in the foster care of Lou Ann and Scott
Mullen, veteran foster parents with an excellent record. The Mullens are a multiracial family: she is Native American; he, "Anglo." In addition to their biological
daughter, the Mullens care for Lou Ann's step-siblings, now 18 and 19, from
Mexico; their adopted former foster child, an 8-year-old bi-racial girl whom they
adopted through a private agency; and several African American foster children.

The Mullens immediately fell in love with Matthew. They stayed up many late
nights comforting him as his little system overcame the drug addiction. When he
was a month old, Lou Ann told DPRS that they wanted to adopt him. "Don't even
think about it," she was told, for Matthew was black and the Mullens were not. (Of
course, Matthew was black when he arrived at their doorstep.) The Mullens made
numerous requests to adopt Matthew but DPRS consistently said "no way," for his
proper place was with a same-race family.

During this period, Matthew's brother Joseph, then four, was living with another foster family. Although DPRS claimed it wanted to place the boys for adoption together, they ignored Lou Ann's request to bring Joseph into the Mullen foster home so that the boys could establish a bond. In fact, over the course of one year, DPRS held only three sibling visits with the boys for a total visitation time of two and a half hours.

After several fruitless searches, DPRS found an African American home to adopt the boys. In August 1994, the agency removed Matthew from the Mullens and Joseph from his foster home, placing them with virtual strangers. DPRS told Lou Ann not to attempt any contact with Matthew.

Matthew's removal devastated the Mullens, who felt as if there had been a death in the family. According to Lou Ann, Matthew used to love to sit by the window every night at dinner and look outside. After DPRS removed him, the only visible sign of his presence was the little handprint that remained on the kitchen window. Lou Ann refused to let anyone wipe it away.

Within seven weeks of placement with the African American family, Matthew and Joseph were returned to DPRS custody when the family had a change of heart. Rather than return Matthew to the Mullens and place Joseph with him, DPRS sent them to an African American foster home, claiming it wanted to keep the boys together. However, when the Mullens asked to adopt both boys, DPRS workers told them they wanted to place them with a black family, "for their culture."

Undeterred, the Mullens persisted in their attempts to adopt the boys and were told they'd be considered with "all the other families." Since DPRS had no other families to consider, the agency conducted recruiting efforts, placing pictures of Matthew and Joseph in newspapers and on television. One newspaper pictured a teary-eyed Matthew and a beaming Joseph under the heading, "Brothers Need Love and Affection." Apparently DPRS thought they needed only the love and affection of an African American family.

While the Mullens' adoption application was pending with DPRS, the foster family then caring for the boys had to be closed down on short notice. Desperate to find someplace to put Matthew and Joseph, DPRS called the Mullens asking if they would take them in on a foster care basis. Lou Ann heartily agreed, although she asked why the placement couldn't be considered a pre-adoptive placement. "No," she was told, "we want to see how they fit in and after six months we may consider you with all the other families." Again, there were no other families, and DPRS continued recruiting. Certain that once a family was found Matthew and Joseph would be removed, the Institute for Justice filed suit on the boys' behalf, challenging the constitutionality of DPRS' conduct. The suit was filed as a class action in the hopes of representing all minority children whose adoption opportunities are impeded by state agencies' commitment to "racematching."

II. Racematching Disproportionally Harms Minority Children

A. *What is Racematching?*

In its most benign form, racematching is simply the practice of placing a child with an adoptive family that reflects the child's racial makeup. That sounds pretty straightforward. In fact, however, racematching by state child welfare agencies takes on a much more pernicious character.

Professor Elizabeth Bartholet at Harvard Law School has conducted a comprehensive investigation of how racematching actually occurs in these agencies -- sometimes in spite of but more often in conformity with written agency policies and state laws.[2] There is a widespread consensus among social workers and agency supervisors that children should be placed with families of the same race. Most state adoption agencies separate their children into "racial pools" reflecting perceived notions about the race of the child.[3] Also, part-black mixed-race children will be classified as African American, even if they are primarily white or of some other racial group.[4]

At the same time, prospective adoptive families are classified into racial pools. When considering adoptive placements for children, agencies will look only at the matching pools of prospective parents, automatically screening out the possibility of an interracial placement or turning to it as a "last resort," where that means years have passed and a same race family hasn't been found.

B. *Statistics*

Racematching has its most detrimental impact on children in the African American and Hispanic (usually Mexican) pools. There are an estimated 500,000 children in the foster care system. Approximately half of these children are free for adoption, which means reunification with the biological family is unfeasible and parental rights have been terminated. Of the children free for adoption, over half of them are considered non-white, and the majority of those are African American. This reveals a startling overrepresentation of African Americans: approximately 40% of the children awaiting a family are black, but blacks make up only about 13% of the general population. The National Adoption Center reports that approximately 67% of the "hard to place" children are black and 26% are white.[5] Yet approximately 67% of the families waiting for children are white, while only 31% are black, and there aren't nearly as many prospective families as there are waiting children.

The point is this: the severe disproportionality in the numbers of waiting minority children and available same race families means that racematching necessarily consigns these children to wait longer -- typically twice as long -- before finding a home. Sometimes it means they never find a permanent home.

C. *What Harm Delay?*

Denial of a home clearly harms children waiting -- but how much delay is harmful? Studies of the adjustment of transracial adoptees compared to same race adoptees show that the single most important factor in their adjustment was the *age* at which they were adopted, not race.[6] Moreover, and perhaps more dangerously, agencies committed to racematching necessarily put minority kids at greater risk of never being adopted, since in general a child's chances for adoption decline with age, dropping off significantly once a child reaches three. Delay begets more delay and as the clock ticks, the minority child's chances for a family plummet. In sum, when the state uses race to hold up adoptions of children in need, race becomes the burden a child must bear, a factor that determines what his or her opportunities in life are going to be.

III. Brief History of Interracial Adoption

For the most part, interracial adoption did not surface in the United States until almost the middle of the century. The first interracial and international adoptions occurred in the aftermath of World War II, which left thousands of homeless children worldwide. Following the Korean war, South Korea made many of its orphaned children available for adoption, many of whose fathers had been American soldiers stationed in Korea during the war.[7]

In the 1960s, there was a dramatic increase in the number of domestic interracial adoptions, a result largely influenced by the civil rights movement and its integrationist ideology. Moreover, the movement called attention to the plight of the many minority children in foster care. In truth, interracial adoption responded to the social and cultural realities of the times: more minority children needed homes as public child welfare agencies faced a burgeoning population of minorities; white adoptive families faced a scarce population of available white children; and the integration sealed the deal. In 1968, 733 children were placed interracially, a figure that more than tripled in the following three years. By 1971, interracial adoptions reached a peak at 2,574.[8]

In 1972, the National Association of Black Social Workers (NABSW) put the brakes on this increase in interracial adoption by disseminating an influential and now (in)famous position paper. Comparing interracial placements to a form of "cultural genocide," the NABSW staked out its position as follows:

> Black children should be placed only with Black families, whether in foster care or for adoption. Black children belong physically, psychologically and culturally in Black families in order that they receive the total sense of themselves and develop a sound projection of their future. Human beings are products of their environment and develop their sense of values, attitudes and self concept within their family structures. Black children in white homes are cut off from the healthy development of themselves as Black people.[9]

In the years following this attack on interracial adoption, the number of such placements plummeted, so that in 1975, only 831 interracial placements were reported.[10]

The NABSW grounded its extreme position in two justifications: First, that only black families could provide black children with the healthy sense of racial identity and self-esteem; second, interracial placements would dilute and eventually lead to the demise of African American culture (hence, "cultural genocide"). As will be discussed in a moment, neither of these justifications[11] has been borne out. Further, the second one, based on the desire to protect the existence of black culture, clearly requires one to stray from the ordinary focus of child placement proceedings, namely, the best interest of the individual child, in favor of perceived benefits to a racial group. That in itself is problematic for anyone who believes that individual rights ought to prevail over collective "rights."

Unfortunately, the NABSW's stance survives today and has had a tremendous impact on the way public child welfare agencies treat interracial placements. And, although in recent media appearances NABSW representatives have claimed that the organization does not oppose interracial placements in *all* circumstances, I participated in a television debate with Leora Neal, an NABSW spokeswoman who, when asked, was unable to identify *any* situation in which she would approve such a placement. In fact, NABSW's 1991 position paper expressly states:

> NABSW herewith reaffirms its position against transracial adoption and continues to take a vehement stand against the placement of African American children in white homes. African American children should NOT be placed with white parents under any circumstances . . . Although many white families applying to adopt African American children probably can provide loving homes and parenting skills, none of them can fulfill African American children's need to feel positive about their African American identity. . . NABSW does not believe the most sensitive, loving and skilled white parent could avoid doing irreparable harm to a[n] African American child.[12]

A. *Research on Interracially Adopted Children as Adults*

In 1972 when the NABSW first sounded its alarm bells about the dangers of interracial adoption, neither the group's proponents nor opponents had much to offer in the way of empirical evidence to support or refute NABSW's claims. In fact, although most of the available studies of interracially adopted children concluded that they were not harmed by such adoptions, critics argued that the studies were useless because they didn't examine the individuals as adults.

By the time NABSW came out with its 1991 statement, its leaders should have known better. Around 1972, sociologists Rita Simon and Howard Altstein began a 20-year longitudinal study comparing children adopted interracially to those adopted by same race families, as well as siblings born into these families. Simon and Altstein revisited their families every four years or so and reevaluated them to assess self-esteem, racial identity, closeness to family, attitudes about race and discrimination, etc. What they found was that the interracially adopted children had in fact developed very healthy and positive attitudes about their racial identity and tended to have a strong sense of self-esteem. Moreover, when these adoptees did encounter discrimination and racial insults, they were able to cope with the problems in a way that did not force them to reject who they were.[13] In other words, the NABSW's predictions have proven erroneous.

With respect to the NABSW's cultural genocide argument, as I noted earlier, it is a collectivist argument and personally I would reject it for that reason. But there's another reason to reject it: it is unfounded. Assume for the sake of argument that interracial placements "dilute" the black culture[14] in which a black child would have participated and to which she would have contributed had she been raised by a black family. Now imagine that all 40,000 black children currently consigned to state foster care were placed interracially. The impact of these placements on the black population as a whole simply does not rise to the level of a real "threat": the 40,000 black children constitute less than one percent of the black population in this country.

Moreover, it seems that those who believe that the state should protect against the demise of racial and ethnic cultures would also support banning interracial marriage, a practice which obviously dilutes the purity of the races, especially when subsequent generations are born.[15] Fortunately, nearly 30 years ago the Supreme Court struck down attempts to prohibit interracial marriage as violative of the Fourteenth Amendment of the U.S. Constitution.[16]

Today, the NABSW still contends that African American children should not be raised by whites, even though the organization has no empirical evidence to support its position. The empirical research that does exist clearly invalidates the NABSW's arguments; further, the literature on child development demonstrates that often the only alternative to interracial placements -- i.e., remaining in foster care and possibly never finding a home -- results in harm to children. And, in fact, rather than address this issue, the NABSW prefers to divert attention away from the empirical evidence that shows that for adopted children, the single most important factor in their adjustment and healthy development is that they are in a loving stable environment as early as possible in their lives.

IV. State Laws, Policies and Practices

A. *State Statutes, Policies and Practices*

Forty-three states require state social workers to use race as a factor in considering placement of a child for adoption. Eleven states and the District of Columbia have adopted racial preference schemes requiring agencies to look for a racial match before considering an interracial placement, even if they have to look nationally and even if a local interracial placement is available.

Until January 1996, California had the most heinous anti-interracial adoption statute: it mandated a waiting period of 90 days before social workers could consider any interracial placements for a child; even after the 90 days had passed, workers were required to document in hideous detail all diligent efforts made to find a same race placement before an interracial placement could be considered. In January 1996, the state enacted a new law that prohibits the use of race as a sole factor in placement decisions, which mirrors the federal Multiethnic Placement Act, discussed below.

Some of these statutes may not seem so horrible on their face, but keep in mind that racial considerations are required in these states regardless of whether a currently available family of a different race wants to adopt the child, even if it is the foster family that has raised her. I met several families in San Diego who had raised different race children in foster care for four and five years and then had tried to adopt them, only to have the state remove the children for adoptive placement with a same race family, whether real or hypothetical.

Further, regardless of the language of a particular state's statute, across the board the policies and practices in these public agencies are virtually identical. In fact, when I began investigating this issue, I virtually ignored looking at Texas because it had a sweeping adoption anti-discrimination statute that prohibited the use of race to delay, deny, or otherwise discriminate in adoptive placements. Yet I kept hearing from foster families in Texas, begging for help because social workers blatantly (and proudly) thwarted that law. I've talked with families around the country, and almost every story I hear is uncanny in its fit in a pattern of discrimination and retaliation by social workers.

B. *Multiethnic Placement Act*

In October 1994, Congress passed a law that was intended to address the problem of the disproportionately high number of minority children languishing in foster homes. The Multiethnic Placement Act,[17] which applies to all state agencies receiving federal funds, proscribes the use of race as the "sole factor" to delay or deny an adoption; however, the statute specifically states that race is a "permissible consideration" along with other factors. In its original form, the Act would have prohibited the use of race altogether to delay or deny an adoption. The apparently minor modification that race can't be the "sole factor" created an exception to the anti-discrimination principle big enough to drive a huge truck through.

As we feared before this modification of the Act was passed, agencies would see the "permissible consideration" language as federal authorization to racematch where no such authorization had existed previously. Indeed, in both of our test cases, which I'll discuss in a moment, the state agencies have asserted that the Multiethnic Placement Act permits the very practices we challenge.

V. Is Racematching Unconstitutional?

There is no dispute that an outright ban on interracial adoption is unconstitutional. A little over twenty years ago, many states in the South still had such statutory bans in place, arising out of the very rationale that enforced segregation and permitted the enactment of Jim Crow laws. However, the last outright ban on interracial adoptions met its demise in Louisiana in 1972. The case of *Compos v. McKeithen*[18] involved a Louisiana statute that prohibited the adoption of a white child by a black and vice-versa. The federal district court declared that the ban violated the equal protection clause of the Fourteenth Amendment and, in its wisdom, held that any hypothetical disadvantages accompanying interracial placements must be compared to the alternative: institutional (foster) care.

Today, the question that still remains open is the extent to which, if at all, race can be used to screen out prospective adoptive families from children who need homes. This is not a frivolous question when you consider that in no other area of public life -- housing, employment, education -- do we tolerate the use of race to flatly deny opportunities to minorities. Even in the affirmative action context,[19] where an aggrieved (usually white) party challenges the denial of opportunities on the basis of race, the viability of programs that permit racial considerations remains open to question following the Supreme Court's 1995 decision in *Adarand Constructors, Inc. v. Pena*[20] and the decision by the Fifth Circuit Court of Appeals in *Hopwood v. Texas*.[21]

Prior to 1984, several lower courts had ruled that the use of race as a factor in an adoption placement decision was constitutionally permissible so long as it was not the sole factor. In 1977, in *Drummond v. Fulton County Dept. of Family & Children's Services*,[22] the Fifth Circuit Court of Appeals held that it was permissible for a Georgia child welfare agency to use race as the determinative factor in removing a mixed race child from his foster family of two years and denying their adoption application, so long as race was not the sole factor. The court went on to say that the "difficulties inherent in interracial adoptions justify making race a relevant factor." It did not describe what these difficulties were, but subsequent empirical evidence and a 1984 Supreme Court decision suggest that although *Drummond* has not been expressly overruled, it is no longer viable.[23] If the inherent difficulties the court was referring to were those suggested by the NABSW, as I noted, the empirical research reveals that these concerns are unfounded.

If the difficulties the court refers to are potential prejudice the child will face in society, the Supreme Court has expressly held that such concerns are illegitimate in deciding a child's placement. In 1984, the Court decided *Palmore v. Sidoti*.[24] In *Palmore*, a white couple had divorced and the mother was awarded custody. Subsequently, the mother moved in with and eventually married a black man. The child's father petitioned the trial court for a change of custody based on the fact that his daughter would face prejudice from living in a racially mixed household. The Supreme Court struck down the decision in sweeping terms. It stated:

> A core purpose of the 14th Amendment was to do away with all governmentally-imposed discrimination based on race. Classifying persons according to their race is more likely to reflect racial prejudice than legitimate public concern; the race, not the person, dictates the category . . . Whatever problems racially mixed households may pose for children in 1984 can no more support a denial of constitutional rights than could the stresses that residential integration was thought to entail in 1917. The reality of private biases and possible injury they might inflict are not permissible considerations under the equal protection clause.[25]

Although opponents of interracial adoptions continue to rely on *Drummond*, I believe that after *Palmore*, the Supreme Court would strike down a case like *Drummond*. Commentators disagree about the application of *Palmore* to an adoption case -- it involved a custody battle between a child's birth parents -- but the breadth of the Court's language and the fact that *Palmore* has been cited in numerous non-custody equal protection cases suggests otherwise. Nevertheless, as noted, *Palmore*'s application to an interracial adoption case has yet to come before the Supreme Court, although the Institute for Justice is currently involved in two test cases, and the possibility of a third one.

The goal of these test cases is to establish a rule of law prohibiting the state from using race to screen out prospective adoption opportunities: in other words, all children available for adoption are entitled to the same adoption opportunities regardless of race. This does not mean that children should be placed with families that do not want them, or vice-versa: it means simply that race should not be used to eliminate otherwise viable opportunities without evaluating the prospective parents and each individual child to determine whether adoption is in the child's best interest.

In Texas, we represent Matthew and Joseph and a class of non-white children in the state's custody who are awaiting adoption.[26] We seek a ruling that the state's racematching policies and practices violate the equal protection rights of these children. In Tennessee, we represent "Baby Jane Doe," a black child whose adoption opportunities are necessarily limited by the fact that the state unabashedly engages in racematching, even though it concedes the virtual impossibility in defining "race."[27]

Both of these cases have put state child welfare agencies on trial, forcing them to account for the fact that they deny adoption opportunities to certain children depending on the racial classifications into which the children fall. As I noted, tolerance for -- and, indeed, the promotion of -- racematching by state agencies appears to be an exception to a general anti-discrimination sentiment in the country. It is an exception that merits our moral outrage, for who else will speak for the children?

End Notes

1. Pearl S. Buck, *Children For Adoption*, p. 91 (1964).
2. Professor Bartholet's findings, and her in-depth analysis on interracial adoption can be found in "Where Do Black Children Belong? The Politics of Racematching in Adoption," 139 *U. Pa. L. Rev.* 1163 (1991). A shorter, slightly different version of this article is found in *Reconstruction*, 22 (1992).
3. "Perceived notions" is the more accurate term because often the child's full racial makeup or ethnicity is unknown and may only become apparent as the child gets older.

4. This practice is an ironic distortion of the "one drop rule" of yore, where one was deemed "Negro" even if his or her black ancestry was a mere fraction of the whole genetic picture. Back then, however, the rule was used by whites to deny legal rights and benefits to blacks; in the adoption context, it is used by those interested in protecting group culture and identity.

5. A "hard to place" child is characterized as such because she is older and/or suffers from some kind of physical, psychological or emotional disability.

6. Feigelman, William and Arnold Silverman, *Chosen Child: New Patterns of Adoptive Relationships*, New York: Praeger, 1983.

7. Bartholet, 139 *U. Pa. L. Rev.* at 1178.

8. Simon, Rita J. and Howard Altstein, *Transracial Adoption*, New York: John Wiley and Son, 1977, p. 30.

9. NABSW 1972 Position Paper, as quoted in Rita J. Simon & Howard Altstein, *Adoption, Race and Identity*, New York: Praeger, 1992, p. 2.

10. Simon and Altstein, *op. cit.*, p. 30.

11. They were actually unfounded predictions.

12. "Preserving African American Families: Research and Action Beyond the Rhetoric," NABSW 1991 Position Paper at 25.

13. The most recent findings of the Simon and Altstein study can be found in Rita J. Simon, Howard Altstein and Marygold Melli, *The Case For Transracial Adoption*, Washington, D.C.: American Univ. Press, 1994.

14. Assume again for the sake of argument that "black culture" is a definable, monolithic entity about which all blacks agree. I reject this contention, as do prominent members of the African American community who support interracial adoption as a way to address the immediate needs of children awaiting adoption. For example, Harvard Law Professor Randall Kennedy and Yale Psychiatrist and Professor of African American Studies Dr. Ezra E.H. Griffith do not believe that blacks agree on what constitutes their "culture" any more than members of other racial or ethnic groups.

15. Professor Jim Chen of the University of Minnesota Law School has written a wonderfully articulate and insightful article on the implications of attempting to prescribe the racial and ethnic composition of families. See *Unloving*, Professor Chen artfully weaves into his article passion for the issue, personal anecdotes, profound insight and clever and compelling writing. Not bad for a law review article.

16. *Loving v. Virginia*, 388 U.S. 1(1967).

17. 42 U.S.C. §§622, 5115a (1994).

18. 341 F.Supp. 264 (E.D. La. 1972).

19. I'm not suggesting that racematching is a form of affirmative action because I don't think it is; affirmative action is remedial and hence, retrospective, while using race to decide adoptive placements is justified in terms of the avoidance of a perceived future harm. Indeed, supporters of affirmative action such as Harvard Law School Professors Elizabeth Bartholet and Laurence Tribe are avid proponents of interracial adoption.

20. 115 S.Ct. 2097 (1995).

21. 1996 WL 120235 (5th Cir. 1996).

22. 563 F2d 1200 (5th Cir. 1977).

23. The Fifth Circuit's *Hopwood* decision, which held that race cannot be used as "a factor" in law school admissions decisions, suggests that *Drummond* is no longer good law.

24. 466 U.S. 429 (1984).

25. *Id.* at 432 (citations omitted).

27. *Baby Jane Doe by and through Reisman v. Tennessee Dept. of Human Services, et al.*, Case No. 93-3083-G (W.D. Tennessee).

The Need for Reform in Federal Welfare Programs: A New Proposal

Ronald K. Henry, Attorney at Law
Washington, D.C.

The best service we can provide to "at-risk" children is to reduce the number of children who become "at-risk." Regardless of the social pathology that is under study, whether it be teenage pregnancy, drug abuse, suicide, low self-esteem, juvenile delinquency, poor academic performance, or any of our other social ills, the greatest causal factor is family breakdown and father absence.

In virtually all of our programs, the phrase "family preservation" has become narrowly defined to mean the propping up of the single mother household as a stand-alone entity. While most single parents do all they can for their children, and many children of single parents develop beautifully, the inescapable history of our programs demonstrates that many single mother households will never succeed as stand-alone units and many children in those households are in grave danger, both physically and developmentally.

The tunnel vision that afflicts current "family preservation" efforts can be seen at all stages of the child welfare process. It is rare for a caseworker even to seek the identity of the child's father and almost unheard of for the caseworker to seek information regarding the father's fitness and willingness to provide for the child's needs. If the father independently comes forward in an effort to assist the child, the caseworker's standard response is to resist all involvement other than cash transfer payments. This resistance is wrong. The government's interest is in protecting the child and not in defending one parent's ownership of that child against all others. "Family preservation" must be understood to include and encourage the participation of fathers and must move beyond the mere administration of programs designed to prop up the single parent as a stand-alone entity.

The absurdity of the current system is even more starkly highlighted in situations where the caseworker realizes that the child must be taken from the care of the single mother. In every state in the country, the standard operating procedure is for the bureaucracy to skip over the father and the entire extended family and consider only third party placement. The bureaucracy's fallacy is in viewing child placement as a simple dichotomy -- an unfit single mother versus third party foster care or adoption.

It is time to reform welfare. We must change the systems under which our only criteria are that beneficiaries must continue to neither work nor marry. Children are harmed when the unintended consequence of policy is to favor non-working, single parent households over all others.

I. Overview of Principles and Programs

There is widespread agreement that the current welfare system is destructive of the families it was intended to help. Despite its good intentions, the government has made a devil's bargain with the poor -- "We will give you money as long as you continue to neither work nor marry." Current programs and many reform proposals are patronizing. They assume that large classes of citizens are simply too stupid and incompetent to make any current or near term contribution to their own support. Real welfare reform requires recognition that there is no respect for the individual unless there is respect for the individual's labor.

A. *"Making Work Pay" Rhetoric and Reality*

Work always pays. Our problem is that we have established a parallel system under which non-work often pays better. Most law abiding citizens work 40 or 45 years to qualify for a Social Security benefit that is smaller than a teenager's welfare package. Many welfare recipients are not unemployed, they are prematurely retired. We have long recognized that Social Security rules discourage paid employment among senior citizens. We have recently recognized that welfare rules discourage paid employment among welfare recipients. The cornerstone of welfare reform must be respect for the importance and dignity of work. Except for the small number of people who are genuinely unable to make any contribution to their own needs, welfare must be a supplement, not a substitute for work.

Welfare reform requires attention to four areas: responsibility, paternity, accountability, and eligibility.

B. *Responsibility*

Responsibility should be immediate, mandatory and universal. Beginning immediately with entry into any welfare program, every recipient should be required to devote 40 hours per week to some combination of job search, training and work, with a strong emphasis on work. Actual work experience is generally the best training for advancement in the workplace. An immediate, universal work requirement also eliminates the "no job" option and encourages serious search efforts for the best available job.

The work requirement can be satisfied by private employment or by unpaid public service in exchange for receipt of the welfare benefit. Work programs should not discriminate against the non-welfare working poor. Vouchers and other special incentives to hire welfare recipients create the risk of displacing other workers. We should not support programs that have the unintended consequence of encouraging people to enter welfare as the path to job preferences. Community service jobs (e.g., assignment to charitable organizations) provide benefits to the community and training to the employees at little or no government cost. Many of the current, unmet needs of communities can be satisfied by this new pool of labor as a supplement to, rather than a substitute for, current employees.

All programs must be open to and end the current discrimination against two parent families. In two parent families, at least one parent must satisfy the 40 hour requirement.

Welfare reform should also begin the process of examining barriers to entry-level job creation. Many worthy tasks in society are not performed because the total cost of obtaining labor, including regulatory and recordkeeping burdens, exceeds the value of the service. We need to examine the extent to which willing workers have been priced out of the market by government mandates.

Child care may be less of a problem than argued by some. Most current working parents utilize some low-cost combination of family, friends and school to satisfy day care needs. As discrimination against two parent households is eliminated, a greater number of children will have access to child care from both parents. Finally, a portion of the community service assignments can be made to child care organizations to increase the available supply at little or no incremental cost. The Head Start Program already utilizes large numbers of low income parents who begin as unpaid interns and progress to paid staff and supervisory positions.

C. Paternity

Current policy fails to distinguish between "runaway" and "thrown away" or "driven away" parents. The federal government spends approximately two billion dollars per year on child support enforcement but purposefully and consciously excludes fathers from all parent-child programs. Under current AFDC rules, the low income father who wishes to be a physical and emotional asset to his children also becomes a financial liability by disqualifying them from most assistance. Research conducted by HHS itself confirms that both mothers and fathers distrust the bureaucracy and work jointly to conceal paternity. We cannot be surprised by low income parents who separate or conceal paternity when our policies make such behavior the economically rational course. A work requirement for single parents and an end to discrimination against two-parent households will change the dynamics of paternity establishment.

Eligibility for all federal programs should require establishment of paternity, beginning with eligibility for the WIC (Women, Infants, and Children) program. That program itself must be revised to develop and encourage the roles of fathers.

Paternity establishment forms in hospital programs should encourage the parties to voluntarily establish custody and visitation as well as financial support. Avoidance of poverty and welfare dependency are directly linked to father involvement. Child support compliance exceeds 90% in joint custody families. Child poverty rates and welfare dependency rates are much lower in father custody families than in mother custody. Women's workforce participation and economic security are increased in joint custody and father custody families.

D. Accountability

AFDC and other programs are intended for the benefit of the dependent children. Adults receive the benefits and are expected to participate in the programs in support of the children's needs. Failure or refusal to participate in required programs or to spend the cash payments for the benefit of the children should be seen as evidence of child neglect or abuse. Such evidence should weigh heavily in determining whether it is in the best interests of the child to transfer custody to a more responsible relative or to consider a foster care placement. Prior efforts at reform have been reluctant to impose sanctions upon uncooperative and irresponsible adults because of a fear of "punishing the child." The reality is that current policies allow children to be held as hostages to guarantee continued subsidy of adult irresponsibility.

All recipients should be required to reimburse the value of benefits received. Currently, child support paid by non-custodial parents is used for reimbursement after a $50 per month waiver. The custodial parent should have the obligation to reimburse one-half of the welfare payments made on behalf of the child and each adult should have the obligation to reimburse benefits paid on behalf of that adult. Many welfare recipients require only short term assistance and that assistance can fairly be treated as a loan or a line of credit rather than as a grant. A uniform reimbursement requirement also encourages all recipients to minimize the period of dependency, take no more benefits than are required, and resume paid employment at the earliest possible date. Community service should be counted toward the reimbursement obligation but should be valued at a level that does not compete with the attractiveness of paid employment.

E. Eligibility

Under the law of each state, parents have an obligation of financial responsibility for their minor children. If the minor children themselves become parents, the minor parents should continue to be the obligation of their own parents. Accordingly, the birth of a child to minor parents may create a requirement for welfare assistance to the new infant but does not create a requirement for assistance to the minor parents unless their own parents are unable to supply the required support. Minor parents must live with or at the expense of their own parents. Payments on behalf of the new infant should be made to the parents of the minor parents as their guardians. Welfare payments should be limited to citizens and immigrants with refugee status. Income based eligibility standards should consider both the income of the parents and any resources that are voluntarily available from the kinship network. Fraud must be addressed as a serious matter. Welfare benefits are based on the applicant's self-reporting of available income. If a person committing welfare fraud has concealed additional income, welfare eligibility must be recalculated, at a minimum, to include the demonstrated capacity for self support. The proposal that follows provides more details. Other fraud reduction mechanisms including electronic transfers and improved identification verification must be adopted.

The earned income tax credit must be modified to reduce the incentive and opportunity for strategies such as over-reporting of income to maximize benefits and to reduce discrimination against two parent families. Currently, many working class couples are ineligible for EITC but, simply by splitting into two dysfunctional fragments, both become eligible.

II. Welfare Eligibility: Kinship Alternatives to Welfare

There is a broad consensus that welfare dependency is not in the best interests of children. Recent legislative initiatives have begun to examine the structural flaws in existing welfare programs. One of the best opportunities for reducing welfare dependency is to be found in the development of more thoughtful eligibility criteria to better identify the children who are actually in need of welfare assistance.

Currently, most welfare programs look only at the cash income of the custodial single parent without regard to the availability of voluntary kinship or extended family assistance. The following proposal provides that welfare eligibility should be determined by examining all resources that are available *voluntarily* through the child's kinship network. It does not relieve the child's parents of their obligations nor does it impose new obligations on other relatives. Only voluntary kinship assistance is considered.

PROPOSED KINSHIP CARE ACT OF 1996

SECTION ONE

Findings and Purposes

The Congress of the United States finds that:

> Welfare programs are intended to provide temporary economic sustenance for individuals while they seek to enter the workforce and eventually extricate themselves and their dependents from poverty.

> Welfare programs have fallen short of this goal as many individuals receiving assistance fail to find and retain jobs.

> The failure to escape poverty persists through generations as children of welfare families go onto welfare rolls as adults, resulting in a needless waste of human potential as well as economic and other costs to society.

> A primary cause of intergenerational welfare dependency is the adverse impact of the welfare environment upon children.

To break intergenerational welfare dependency requires, where possible, the separation of children from the welfare environment and their placement into family situations that will be conducive to rejection of the welfare career.

Current welfare provisions lack measures that would assist in the elimination of intergenerational welfare dependency and, indeed, actually encourage such dependency by ignoring the availability of non-welfare alternatives for dependent children.

It is therefore in the public interest to amend the welfare laws to eliminate the encouragement of intergenerational welfare dependency and to promote the placement of children in non-welfare environments more conducive to an economically and socially productive adulthood.

SECTION TWO

A. Eligibility

No person shall be eligible to receive benefits under this program by reason of the need of that person to support one or more child dependents unless the administrator *[or agency or other appropriate state official]* has certified, after undertaking diligent efforts, that there are no family members who are fit and willing to provide for the needs of such children without resort to welfare dependency. Such certification shall be required prior to initial entry into the program and, thereafter, upon periodic reviews of eligibility conducted annually.

B. Teenage Parents - Welfare Eligibility

Under the law of each state, parents have an obligation of financial responsibility for their own minor children. If the minor children themselves become parents, these minor parents should continue to be the obligation of their own parents.

Current welfare eligibility rules subvert this basic rule of parental responsibility and create perverse incentives for teenage childbearing. Simply by having a child, federal programs give the teenager an independent income source and relieve the teenager's parents of the obligations imposed by state law.

Under state law, a minor must live with or at the expense of his or her own parents. The birth of a child to that minor should not be a basis for the federal government to override state law. The federal government should not subsidize the establishment of independent households by minors.

If the parents of the minor are already on public assistance, their payments should be governed by the rules applicable to other families experiencing the birth of an additional dependent. If the parents of the minor are a danger to the minor or grandchild, the case should be processed under the normal rules of guardianship used by the state. Again, there is no justification for a federal program which automatically establishes all minors as independent households upon the birth of a baby.

SECTION THREE

Divorced Families - Dependent Tax Exemption

Prior law provided that the dependent exemption for a child of divorced parents was available to the parent providing greater than 50% of the child's support. At that time, it was difficult to determine which parent provided greater than 50% of the support and the law was changed in 1984 to create a presumption that the exemption would be given to the custodial parent. The current law has created some new problems and has not kept pace with federally imposed changes in the establishment of child support orders.

Most divorce litigants do not have lawyers and, even with lawyers, most divorce decrees fail to address the allocation of the dependent tax exemption. Some courts have taken the position that they do not have authority to allocate the exemption to the non-custodial parent even in cases where the custodial parent is unemployed and it is clear that the non-custodian is providing 100% of the child's financial support. Allocating the dependent exemption to a household with no income does not help the child and, in fact, reduces the after-tax income available to support the child.

Recent federal legislation governing the establishment of child support orders has eliminated the uncertainty which motivated the 1984 law regarding allocation of the dependent exemption. In the past, child support orders were subjective, *ad hoc* determinations that did not identify each parent's share of the child's financial costs. Federal law now requires that each state have a presumptive, mathematical guideline for the establishment of child support. Under the "income shares" model used by most states, the state determines a child's costs and then allocates these costs in proportion to each parent's income. The child support computation formula thus establishes unambiguously which parent provides more than 50% of the child's financial support.

The law should be revised to provide that the dependent exemption shall be allocated to the parent who bears more than 50% of the child's financial support as established by the applicable child support order. To avoid ambiguity and dispute, the taxpayer claiming the exemption could be required to submit a copy of the court order as an attachment to the tax return. Most child support orders are now generated by computers using the state's child support formula and are set forth in a one page computer printout.

SECTION FOUR

Responding to Welfare Fraud

In the District of Columbia and in most states, welfare fraud is a no-risk adventure.

If caught, *the standard guilty plea merely requires restitution (sometimes only partial) which is paid out of future welfare benefits!* Welfare is a disastrously anti-family program in which the government offers itself as a substitute for responsible two-parent family behavior. Welfare fraud multiplies the problem by making welfare more lucrative.

Welfare benefits are predicated on the assumption that the welfare recipient cannot earn an outside income and that a government subsidy is required for basic needs. Initially, we accept the applicant's unilateral assertion of this inability to earn an income. In the case of the welfare cheat, however, behavior proves that an income can be earned and the receipt of welfare benefits is simply a theft of benefits that are not needed. Having proved that an income can be earned, the welfare cheat should be disqualified from receiving benefits *in the future* at least to the extent of the earnings potential that has been demonstrated.

Past enforcement efforts have been backward. The welfare cheat is permitted to quit the unreported job and go back to the dole. The reverse should be true. Having demonstrated earning capacity, the welfare cheat should be disqualified from again asserting an inability to earn income.

In the current economic crisis of budget deficits and soaring welfare rolls, it may finally be possible to impose serious sanctions upon welfare cheaters. The following legislative suggestions are offered:

1.   The presence of unreported income means that the welfare cheat either does not need or has less need for welfare. Accordingly, the law should provide that welfare benefits will be reduced or eliminated on a *forward-going basis* to reflect the income that was being earned during the fraud and thus can be earned in the future.

2.   State laws providing for mandatory jail terms of not less than 30 days for all persons convicted of welfare fraud should be required as a condition for a state's receipt of federal funds.

3.   State laws providing that conviction for welfare fraud is a sufficient basis to support a judicial finding that it is in the best interests of the child for custody to be placed with another relative should be required as a condition for a state's receipt of federal funds.

4.   State laws providing that conviction for welfare fraud is a sufficient basis to support a judicial finding of neglect or abuse so that the child may be placed in foster care should be required as a condition for a state's receipt of federal funds.

Sexual Equality in Custody and Child Support: Now Mothers Can Be Deadbeats Too

Anne P. Mitchell, Attorney at Law,
Palo Alto, CA

One cannot have a meaningful dialogue about the rights and responsibilities of one sex, without also discussing the rights and responsibilities of the other, as they are almost always closely intertwined.

Nowhere is this point more devastatingly driven home than in the area of family law, where our children serve as the fulcrum upon which the competing interests of man and woman are balanced.

My observations are based not just on my background in advocacy for fathers, but on my experiences in another role: as a divorced single mother. Now, here are two things which you will rarely hear a woman admit to: First, the process of divorce, and going through the family law system, can be one of the single most empowering experiences a woman can go through. For the most part, women come to know that they will get the kids, and men will pay for the "pleasure" of being reduced to being a "visitor" in their children's lives. Second, the current feminist elite has no desire for there to be even a semblance of equality in this system, and may in fact be coercing today's woman out of the workforce and back into the nursery.

Out of financial independence, and into financial dependence -- on men. This is all being done in the name of the maternal bond and which, the tradition holds, is a special and somehow magical connection that transcends mere relationship. It is, somehow, an inseverable umbilicus -- something not to be tampered or interfered with -- something sacred.

The Mother-Child Bond

Of course, this can only mean that women must be primary caretakers, which in turn means that men must be their financial benefactors. Or, put more simply: women get the kids, men get to pay.

In fact, even in those rare instances when the men get the kids, the men still get to pay! Consider these figures released in September of 1995 by the Federal Bureau of Census. The picture they paint is one of a blatant bias, and great inequity in our system and society. Moreover, they evidence a high degree of concern for maternal entitlement, with little for the needs of the children for involvement with both parents, and none whatsoever for the status of the fathers, even when they are the custodial parent!

This study reveals that while 27.5% of noncustodial mothers have no timeshare privileges, 42% of noncustodial fathers have no timeshare privileges. Custodial mothers consistently receive higher child support awards than custodial fathers.

Noncustodial mothers go "deadbeat" more frequently than noncustodial fathers.

Noncustodial mothers go "deadbeat" more frequently than noncustodial fathers. In 1991, nearly 24% of custodial mothers got no support. But 37% of custodial fathers received no support. And it gets worse.

Of all custodial parents, both mothers and fathers, below the poverty level, mothers received at least some child support more than 70% of the time. Fathers below the poverty level received NO support more than 75% of the time!

Mothers below the poverty level received full support 41.4% of the time; fathers below the poverty level received full support only 3.5% of the time!

Where is the public outcry against deadbeat moms? There is no outcry, because this is about a maternal subsidy, not about supporting the children.

Unfortunately, many men have also bought into the myth of the maternal bond. Studies show that at least a third of all fathers ask for less custody than they really want, even though they feel as strongly about custody as do mothers. Why do men routinely ask for less time with their children then they really want, leaving the majority of custody to the mother? Because they too have come to believe in the tradition of the sacred mother-child bond, and thus they believe that they are incapable of providing that somehow unique form of nurturing required by their children. Hence, these fathers conclude that the children belong with their mother -- indeed, are better off with their mother -- instead of their inept and unnurturing father selves.

Is it any wonder that these fathers doubt their capacity to nurture their children, given that this is the message provided to them at every turn? It is the subtext of the maternal bond doctrine, as well as an implicit assumption upon which is based the message that "good" fathers are those who provide a maternal subsidy so that their children may remain with their mothers.

And thus the myth is perpetuated. And the women get the children. And the men get to pay. And it is good. For nobody.

We must bring the system back into balance; we must stop, once again, damning women for their choices, and enslaving them with their "virtues."

And then, and only then, will we be able to bring about true equality in our family law system, for then it will no longer be "the woman gets the kids, the man gets to pay," but "the kids get two parents, each of whom are independent and self-sufficient."

The Role of Social Science Data on Public Policy Issues

Rita J. Simon, University Professor
School of Public Affairs and the Washington College of Law,
American University, Washington, D.C.

This essay has four themes that illustrate how social science data are either ignored, distorted, or made up on matters that have significant implications for public policy. The first describes and deplores the current claim that data and research do not matter. For example, this is the latest argument in the debate about transracial adoption (TRA). Family preservation has become the rallying cry and research findings have been declared irrelevant. Spokespersons for the National Association of Black Social Workers (NABSW) have been strongly opposed to transracial adoptions at least since 1971, when their, then-President William Merrit referred to the practice as racial genocide. Over the years the NABSW has altered its rhetoric; racial genocide has became cultural genocide. It also warned some twenty years ago that "it is too early to assess whether TRA serves the children's best interests; wait until the children reach adolescence." Ten years later, the cry shifted to "Wait until they are adults." Today, almost 25 years after the first charges of racial genocide were hurled, the attack against TRA is that "research findings are irrelevant."

What has happened in the intervening years is that a good deal of research has been carried out on the issue; and all of the data show that transracial adoption clearly satisfies the "best interest of the child" standard.[1] They show that transracial adoptees grow up emotionally and socially adjusted, and aware of and comfortable with their racial identities. They perceive themselves as integral parts of their adopted families, and they expect to retain strong ties to their parents and siblings in the future.

The Simon-Altstein study followed families who had adopted children of different races for 20 years. In our last contacts with the families in the study, we reported that the adult black adoptees stressed their comfort with their identities and their awareness that although they may speak, dress, and have different tastes in music than some other blacks, "the African American is wonderfully diverse." One black young woman said: "I feel lucky to have been adopted when I was very young [24 days]. I was brought up to be self-confident -- to be the best I can. I was raised in an honest environment." Another black male said: "I was brought up without prejudice. The experience is fulfilling and enriching for parents and children."

When given the opportunity to express their views on transracial adoption, most people -- black and white -- support it. For example, in January 1991, *CBS This Morning* reported the results of a poll it conducted that asked 975 adults, "Should race be a factor in adoption?" Seventy percent of white Americans said "no," and 71 percent of African Americans said "no." These percentages are the same as those reported by Gallup in 1971 when it asked a national sample the same question.

Opponents of TRA do not provide data that contradict these findings; instead they declare data and research findings to be irrelevant. In the name of family preservation, children remain in foster care and in institutions waiting for birth parents who are in prison, who have a drug problem, who have abused their children, to get over, or work out their problems, so that the biological family can be "preserved." These actions do not serve the children's best interests.

A second theme bears on the issue of "made up" data or references to non-existent data to support the adoption of new laws or policies. A good example of this phenomenon is the claim that there is a direct connection between pornography and violent crimes, therefore pornography should be censored. My assessment of the evidence supports the conclusions reported by Jonathan Rauch in *Kindly Inquisitors* that "no respectable study or evidence has shown any causal link between pornography and actual violence."[2] This argument is the mirror image of the first. Here advocates claim their argument is supported and strengthened by empirical findings when in fact no data exist.

A third theme is the increasing tendency toward evaluating and interpreting data through politicized eyes. On this issue, I refer to the relative involvement of criminal activities. In essence, the radical feminists argue that women who commit the same crimes as men, e.g. embezzlement, larceny, fraud, do it for noble reasons unlike men whose actions are driven by greed, ambition and/or anger. The most recent data (statistics are collected annually by the FBI on a national basis) show that women account for 42% of arrests for fraud, 39% for embezzlement and 32% of larceny. Over a thirty year period there has been a steady and consistent increase in the percentage of women arrested for these property and white collar offenses. For example, in 1963 women accounted for 17% of all arrests for fraud, 19% for embezzlement and 19% for larceny. In 1973, the percentages of female arrests for those crimes were 24, 31, and 30; and in 1983 they were 32, 40, and 31. No such increases occurred among women for violent offenses. In 1963 women accounted for 11.7% of all arrests for violent offenses; in 1973, they accounted for 10.2%; in 1983, for 10.8%; and in 1993, for 12%.

How might we account for these sharp and consistent increases in women's involvement in property and white-collar crimes over the past three decades that are not part of a generally greater increase in criminal activities among women? The "opportunity thesis" that I first spelled out in my 1975 book *Women and Crime* and updated in 1989 in *The Crimes Women Commit, The Punishments They Receive* pulls together and makes sense of these statistical trends.[3] In essence, the arguments state that women are neither more nor less moral than men. Neither are they more nor less inclined to engage in criminal acts. Rather, I argue that opportunities, skills, and social networks historically have contributed to men's propensity to commit crimes and these same factors have limited women's opportunities.

Labor force participation is crucial. A wide range of property offenses can be committed only by persons who have access to other people's money and the skills to manipulate funds. Thus, crimes such as larceny, theft, embezzlement, and fraud are likely to be committed by persons who are in the labor force and who have certain positions in the labor force; and not by full-time homemakers and mothers. The opportunity thesis also predicts a relationship between the position one occupies in the labor force and the opportunities for committing various types of offenses. Executives, managers, and professionals such as accountants and attorneys have opportunities to embezzle much larger sums than do secretaries, bank tellers, bookkeepers and clerks.

What do the data tell us about women's labor force participation? In 1963, 41% of single women and 34.6% of married women were in the labor force. In 1973, the percentages increased to 55.9 and 42.8; in 1983 to 62.6 and 52.3; and in 1993 to 64.7 and 59.3. Not only has the percentage of women in the labor force steadily and consistently increased in the past 30 years, but the type of work they do is also changing. In 1992, 47.3% of all persons in management and professional specialties were women, compared to 17.4% in 1960, 33.9% in 1970, and 40.9% in 1983.

Thus, as more women move into higher status managerial positions, especially those involving expert knowledge and skills, they have more opportunities to commit the types of employment related crimes committed by men. Some women take advantage of these opportunities, just as some men do.

On this issue there are no disagreements about the existence of, or what the data say. The disagreements center on the interpretations. Feminist criminologists argue that the explanations for why women commit property offenses do not apply to men. Women steal, defraud and embezzle to feed hungry children, to maintain their families, and to keep themselves afloat. Men commit these same acts out of greed, ambition and lack of respect for the law.

The fourth theme is that historical facts do not matter. The claims here are that there is nothing to be learned by examining the same phenomenon in the past because the present has no connection to the past. A good example of this theme is the debate about whether immigrants have been good or bad for the United States and whether we should admit more or fewer, now. On this issue, the scenario looks like this: While we proudly refer to ourselves as a country of immigrants, national poll data for the past fifty years show that a large majority of the public is either ambivalent or holds strongly anti-immigrant sentiments. We tend to view immigrants with rose-colored glasses turned backwards. Data support an interpretation which states that those immigrants who came earlier, whenever earlier happens to be, have been good for this country. But those who are coming now, whenever now is, are viewed at best with ambivalence, and more likely with distrust, fear and hostility.

For example, although there were riots in New York, Boston, and Philadelphia when the Irish started coming in large numbers in the 1850s, when the public was asked almost a century and a half later to indicate whether different groups of immigrants have been good for this country, the Irish ranked second highest, just below the English, as having been good for this country. Further, results of national polls conducted between 1982 and 1993 show that the Italians, Jews, Poles and Chinese also were perceived as having been a good thing for this country. But during the period in which they were arriving in great numbers in the last decades of the 19th century and the first two decades of the 20th century, statements such as the following were made about them:

> The entrance into our political, social and industrial life of such vast masses of peasantry, degraded below our utmost conceptions, is a matter which no intelligent patriot can look upon without the gravest apprehension and alarm. These people have no history behind them which is of a nature to encouragement. They have none of the inherited instincts and tendencies which made it comparatively easy to deal with the immigration of the older time. They are beaten men from beaten races. Representing the worst failures in the struggle for existence. Centuries are against them, as centuries were on the side of those who formerly came to us. They have none of the ideas and aptitudes which fit men to take up readily and easily the problem of self care and self government, such as belong to those who are descended from the tribes that met under the oak trees of old Germany to make laws and choose chieftains.[4]

In today's light, these earlier immigrants from Southern and Eastern Europe are viewed as having made positive contributions to American society. The Chinese, against whom we passed special legislation (Chinese Exclusion Act, 1882) that barred all foreign born Chinese from acquiring U.S. citizenship, are also viewed in a positive light. But reversal from a positive to a negative contribution occurs when the public is asked to evaluate immigrants who are currently entering the United States in large numbers. Those groups are consistently perceived as more of a bad than a good thing for the United States. Thus today the Haitians, the Koreans and the Cubans are perceived as especially bad.

Maybe former University of Chicago Professor of Economics and later U.S. Senator from Illinois, Paul Douglas, said it best in 1919 when commenting on this tendency, he wrote: "It is the custom of each generation to view immigrants of its day as inferior to the stock that once came over."[5]

Concluding Comments

It is one thing to select problems one wants to work on because of one's political interests, race, religion, and/or gender. But those factors should not determine the research design or the interpretation of the data. The above characteristics or factors might also influence the implications the researcher sees the findings having on such issues as the level of conflict, the degree of integration, the likelihood of peace, etc. Thus, I am not claiming that the researcher's experiences, demographic characteristics and biography should have no bearing on research. They are likely to be important in the problems she chooses to work on, perhaps also on how he chooses to study the problem (e.g. some will have greater need to do more "hands on" or "observational studies") and in the policy recommendations she chooses to make on the basis of the results. But such "old fashioned" ideas as reliable and valid methods, as cumulative knowledge, as studies being the building blocks for new research, let's hope and work for these principles to survive and flourish.

End Notes

1. The following are major studies conducted between 1971 and 1994: Lucille J. Grow and Deborah Shapiro, *Black Children, White Parents: A Study of Transracial Adoption.* New York: Child Welfare League of America, 1974; Joyce Ladner, *Mixed Families.* New York: Anchor Press, Doubleday, 1977; Ruth G. McRoy and Louis A. Zurcher, *Transracial and Inracial Adoptees: The Adolescent Years.* Springfield, IL: Charles C. Thomas, 1993; Richard Barth and Marian Berry, *Adoption and Disruption.* New York: Aldine de Gruyter, 1988; Rita J. Simon and Howard Altstein, *Adoption, Race and Identity.* New York: Praeger, 1992; and Rita J. Simon, Howard Altstein and Marygold S. Melli, *The Case for Transracial Adoption,* Washington, D.C.: American University, 1994.

2. Jonathan Rauch, *Kindly Inquisitors.* Chicago, IL: University of Chicago Press, 1993, p. 13.

3. Rita J. Simon, *Women and Crime.* NIMH Monograph, Center for Crime and Delinquency, 1975. Also Lexington Books, 1975; Rita J. Simon with Jean Landis, *The Crimes Women Commit, The Punishments They Receive.* Lexington, 1991.

4. Francis Walker, Commissioner General of the Immigration Service, *The Atlantic Monthly,* June 1886.

5. Paul H. Douglas, "Is the New Immigration More Unskilled Than the Old?" *Journal of the American Statistical Association,* Vol. 46, June 1919.

Understanding Differences in the Estimates of Rape from Self-Report Surveys

James P. Lynch, Associate Professor
Department of Justice, Law and Society
American University, Washington, D.C.

Introduction

Estimates of the incidence of rape vary wildly[1] and this variability has generated a great deal of controversy about the extent of this problem. Advocates of legislation to reduce and redress violence against women have cited the higher figures, while opponents of these bills have used the lower estimates.[2] The result has been not only a vitriolic and largely ideological debate over the extent of rape and the need for the bill, but also the trashing of social statistics customarily used to inform these discussions.[3] This "deconstruction" of social statistics from both ends of the ideological spectrum is dangerous. It undermines public confidence in social statistics and concedes policy debates to anecdote and ideology. This is not to deny that there are substantial difficulties in the measurement of rape, but many of these problems can be fixed or otherwise taken into account. It is better for all concerned that we seek to understand why these estimates of the incidence of rape differ than to abandon these flawed statistics for even more deficient forms of evidence.

To date, discussions of why the statistics on the incidence of rape diverge have taken the form of an advocate from one side of the debate critiquing the data presented by the other side. As a result these criticisms have lacked balance and a sense of proportion.[4] They have been selective in terms of the sources of error and divergence that they include and they have seldom been informed by parallel analyses of the data from the statistical series that produce the discrepant estimates. As a result, these exchanges do not specify the magnitude of the errors that they *do* identify and it is very difficult to separate the trivial problems from the more consequential.

This paper explores the question of why we should have such widely diverging estimates of the level of rape. It attempts to present a reasonably complete and balanced picture of the types of errors and non-uniformities that can affect the various methodologies, drawing from the literature on retrospective surveys and especially victimization surveys. Analyses are proposed to estimate the direction and magnitude of errors in each method.

Approaches to Measuring the Incidence of Rape

This discussion focuses on estimates of rape from self-report household surveys. Other methodologies have been used to collect data on rape and attempted rape, principally administrative records systems. The Uniform Crime Reports (UCR) is the best known administrative series that provides estimates of the incidence of rape. In this data system events reported to local police departments are subsequently recorded and reported to the state and ultimately to the Federal Bureau of Investigation (FBI),[5] where these reports are aggregated to estimate the level of rape nationally each year. The common wisdom is that since administrative series require victims to take the initiative to report an event to some authorities and that these authorities must, in turn, record and report these incidents, they will underestimate the incidence of rape and attempted rape.[6] There is good reason, then, to believe that these crimes will be more completely reported in self-report surveys than in these administrative series of official records.[7]

Despite the desirability of self-report surveys relative to existing administrative series, there is evidence that the recounting of events in retrospective surveys also results in substantial under-reporting.[8] This is the case for a wide variety of events, from consumer expenditures to health care to crime.[9] In addition to these recounting problems generic to retrospective surveys, surveys of rape victimization have the additional complexities of identifying events that some respondents are reluctant to divulge and that are sometimes ambiguous.[10] All of this makes measurement of rape difficult.

Specific Survey Designs Used to Assess the Incidence of Rape

The most often cited data on the incidence of rape come from work done by the Bureau of Justice Statistics (BJS) -- the National Crime Survey (NCS) and the National Crime Victimization Survey (NCVS); and by Dean Kilpatrick and his colleagues at the University of South Carolina -- the National Women's Study (NWS). The surveys used by these researchers have very different designs (described briefly in Table 1) that yield radically different estimates of the level of rape. (Figure 1)

Figure 1

Comparison of Rape Incidence and Prevalence Estimates from Different Self-Report Surveys
National Crime Survey
140,000
National Crime Victimization Survey
370,000
National Women's Study
683,000

The NCS and NCVS counts are the number of rape incidents and the NWS counts are prevalence estimates for women 18 to 34. This difference makes it all the more surprising that the NWS estimates are so much greater than the NCVS estimates.

NCS. The BJS estimates of rape during the period 1973 to 1991 came from the NCS. This was a survey of approximately 50,000 households conducted annually by the Census Bureau for the Department of Justice. The survey employed a rotating panel design of housing units. Each unit was in the sample for three and one-half years. The interviews with all persons 12 and older in a household were bounded using the previous interview as a bound for subsequent interviews. The interview included a screening interview and an incident form. The cuing strategy was that of traditional survey interviewing -- screening questions are asked in simple and syntactically correct sentences. There was no intentional redundancy. Most importantly, the survey does not ask directly about rape.[11] If respondents acknowledged an assault and offered that this assault was a rape or a threat of rape then the event would be recorded as a rape in the survey. The predominate mode of interviewing changed over the life of the survey from virtually all in-person interviews in 1973 to largely telephone interviewing in 1991. The NCS employed a six month reference period.

NCVS. In 1991 a radically changed design was introduced into the NCS.[12] The post-1991 NCS is referred to as the NCVS. This new design retained many of the features of the old survey. It was still a rotating panel design and the bounding procedure, the reference period, and the screener/incident form format remained the same. The major design change occurred in the cuing strategy used in the screening interview. Specifically, questions were added to the survey which asked respondents directly about rape and sexual assault. The traditional method of cuing was replaced by a "short cue" screener. This screening interview employed an initial question about the criminal act, e.g. being hit or threatened, followed by a series of short cues that were intended to both clarify the concept and stimulate the respondent's memory by cuing other attributes of the event. A more detailed description of the NCVS screening procedures is presented in Appendix 1. In addition to changes in the cuing strategy, the changes introduced in 1991 included a different method for handling "series" incidents[13] and a maximum use of Computer Assisted Telephone Interviewing (CATI). The introduction of this package of changes produced a 40% increase in the reporting of crimes in the NCVS over that reported in the NCS. The increase for rape was approximately 250%.[14]

NWS. The most often cited estimates of rape not produced by BJS and the Census Bureau come from a study done by Dean Kilpatrick and his colleagues for the National Victims Center and the National Institute of Drug Abuse (NIDA).[15] This was a longitudinal survey of women 18 years of age and older. It was conducted on a nationally representative sample of 2008 women with a 2,000 over-sample of women 18 to 34. Respondents were interviewed three times. The first interview was unbounded, but the second and third interviews were bounded by the previous interview. Two reference periods were employed. In the first interview respondents were asked to report on their experiences over their lifetimes and in the second interview they were asked to report for the year since the first interview. The annual estimates of the prevalence of rape were produced with the data from this second interview. The screening for rape events was done in the context of a much longer interview on trauma and drug use. Screening questions were asked of respondents and those reporting eligible incidents were skipped into a sequence of questions about the attributes of the event. The cuing strategy featured traditional approaches to asking questions, that is, long syntactically correct sentences and the avoidance of redundancy. The screening questions, however, differed from the NCVS in that they asked explicitly about behavior that fit the definition of rape and sexual assault rather than using the term rape. (For a more detailed description of the screening strategies used in the Kilpatrick study see Appendix 2.)

Evaluating Sources of Divergence in the Estimates

There are a number of features of the NCS design that reduced the reporting of rape incidents. Most important of these is the fact that interviewers did not ask respondents directly about their rape experiences. If in response to a question on assaults, the respondents offered that they had been raped, the event would be captured in the survey. This alone would lead one to expect that the NCS estimates substantially under-represented rape and attempted rape relative to the other surveys reviewed in this paper. The large increases in the reports of rape with the introduction of direct questions about rape in the NCVS provide further support for the charge that the NCS estimates were very low. They should not be used to estimate the level of rape and attempted rape. It is less clear how useful these data are for estimating change in the level of these crimes.

The more puzzling question is why the NWS rates should be so much higher than those from the NCVS (See Figure 1). The two designs are similar in some respects. Moreover, Kilpatrick's survey differs from the NCVS in many ways that should depress rather than increase reporting of rape and attempted rape. Specific design differences and their likely effects on the divergence of the rate estimates are discussed below.

Table 1 Description of Survey Designs Used to Estimate the Incidence and Prevalence of Rape

Design Attribute	NCS	NCVS	KILPATRICK
Sample design	Multistage, cluster sample of addresses, nationally representative N=50,0000 hh; 110,000 persons	Multistage, cluster sample of addresses, nationally representative N=50,000 hh; 110,000 persons	Stratified random sample of telephone numbers N=4,008 women
Scope	Estimates of serious common law crime including rape for persons 12 and older	Estimates of serious common law crime including rape & sexual assault for persons 12 and older	Estimates or rape and sexual assault for women 18 and older
Reference period	Six months	Six months	One year
Bounding status	Bounded	Bounded	Bounded
Cuing strategy	Traditional, indirect, narrow net	Short cue, direct, broad net	Traditional, direct, narrow net
Screener/incident form	Yes	Yes	Yes
Mode	Mixed mode; telephone and in person	Mixed mode; telephone and in person	Telephone
CATI	No	Yes (30% of sample)	Yes (100% of sample)
Handling of repeat victimization	Series victimization procedure 3 plus/not in estimates	Series victimization procedure 5 plus/not in estimates	No series victimization procedure
Context	Crime Victimization	Crime Victimization	Drug use, trauma and crime victimization

Populations and Samples. The NWS and the NCVS have slightly different target populations. The former sampled women 18 years of age and older, while the latter included persons 12 years of age and older residing in households. It is not clear what this difference in target populations will mean for the estimates. There are some data from police records suggesting that the prevalence of rape is higher for persons under 18 than for persons over 18. The selectivity in reporting to the police is very great, however, and this limits our ability to apply these data to self-report measures of rape.

The NCVS uses Census address lists as a sampling frame while the NWS employed a telephone frame in sampling their target population. While the vast majority of interviews in the NCVS are conducted by phone, some portion of the interviews are conducted in-person for households without telephones. These non-telephone households are not included in the NWS frame. In general, non-telephone households have higher rates of victimization than households with telephones and this should increase the rape rates from the NCVS relative to the NWS.

Bounding. The two surveys are similar in that they employ bounded interviews. This procedure has been found to be effective in reducing the reporting of events that happened prior to the reference period as occurring in the reference period. Unbounded interviews will result in higher rates due to the telescoping of events into the reference period. If this design feature is constant across both the NCVS and the NWS, it should not contribute to the differences in the resulting estimates. There is some indication, however, that the bounding procedures in the two surveys differ in important respects.

The bounding procedure in the NCVS relies on both a cognitive and a mechanical process. The first interview provides a cognitive bound in that it affords a reference point that the respondent can use to identify recalled events as being outside the reference period and therefore ineligible. Biderman and Cantor (1984) argue that the cognitive aspect of bounding is really an education effect wherein the respondent learns in the first interview that the interviewer is interested in specific events and not expressive behavior. The very detailed information asked for on the incident form (including the date of the incident) impresses upon the respondent the need for accuracy and specificity. In addition to these cognitive effects in which the respondent self-censors, there is a mechanical aspect to bounding in which interviewers eliminate events from out of the reference period. The Census interviewer compares any mention of an event in a second or subsequent interview with the events reported in the prior interview that are listed on the control card. If two similar events are reported, the interviewer asks the respondent if the victimization reported in the current interview was the same event reported in a prior interview. Events identified as the same incident are deleted.

The NWS did re-interview respondents who were interviewed previously and the first interview was used to mark the far bound of the reference period in the second interview. It is plausible to assume, then, that the cognitive effects of bounding may be reasonably similar across the two designs. It is less clear that the mechanical aspects of the Census bounding process were employed in the NWS design. This would increase the NWS rates by including events from outside the reference year in the estimates. Biderman and Cantor's work (1984), however, suggests that the effect on incident rates of differences in mechanical bounding across the two designs will be slight.

Another difference in the bounding procedures in the two surveys is that some portion of the NCVS interviews are unbounded in any given year, while all of the NWS interviews are bounded. This difference occurs because between 14 and 18% of NCVS interviews are conducted with persons moving into sample housing units and who, therefore, have no prior or bounding interview. Since unbounded interviews yield more reports of victimization than bounded interviews, the use of unbounded interviews in annual incident rates from the NCVS should increase these estimates relative to those from the NWS. This difference in bounding procedures, however, will not have a large effect on the differences in the rates.

Longitudinal Components. The surveys are also similar in that both have longitudinal components, but these longitudinal components are somewhat different. The NCVS is a longitudinal design of housing units, while the NWS is a longitudinal design of persons. Respondents in the NCVS can be interviewed up to seven times, while respondents in the NWS are eligible for three interviews. More specifically, since the NWS data used to produce the most cited annual estimate of rape comes from the second wave of interviews, respondents can only be interviewed twice. Analyses of data on the productivity of repeated interviews indicate that the number of repeat interviews is negatively related to mentions of target events. This is referred to as time-in-sample bias. Although respondents in the NCVS are interviewed more often than those in the NWS, the time-in-sample effects should not differ greatly across the designs. This is due to the fact that because of movements in and out of sample units, only about 30% of the NCVS sample is interviewed seven times. Moreover, since most of the decrease in reporting occurs between the first and second interviews, the fact that the NCVS sample has a substantial number of respondents who have been interviewed more than two times will not increase the effects of time-in-sample much relative to the NWS.

The longitudinal nature of these designs also means that they can be affected by attrition, but this too will differ across the two surveys. In the NCVS the persons leaving sample housing units will be replaced by persons moving into the sample. If in-movers are similar to out-movers, then attrition (more aptly called mobility in this case) in the sample should not affect estimates. Since the NWS is a longitudinal design of persons, out-movers are not replaced by in-movers. Consequently, attrition could affect NWS estimates. Moreover, attrition is quite large in the NWS. Approximately 85% of eligible respondents contacted agreed to participate in the first interview and of those 81% agreed to participate in the second (the bounded) interview. The total attrition rate is 32%.

Presumably, attrition in the NWS should result in higher risk individuals leaving the sample. Younger and more mobile people are more likely to leave the sample than other groups and these respondents are also more likely to be victims generally. Also, moving itself seems to contribute to the risk of victimization. If the attrition is due largely to residential mobility and the common wisdom about mobile populations and victimization is true, we would expect that attrition would decrease the rates of reported rapes in the NWS relative to the NCVS. If, on the other hand, attrition in the NWS is due more to refusals than residential mobility, then attrition could increase reporting in the NWS relative to the NCVS. Refusals in the first and the second NWS interviews could be related to an unwillingness to talk about sexual matters generally due to inexperience. This is plausible especially in light of the very explicit cues used in the NWS screening questions. If the probability of rape is related to sexual experience, then refusals may have lower rates of rape and attempted rape than those who agreed to continue participation.

This would cause the NWS to produce higher estimates of rape and sexual assault relative to the NCVS.

Reference Period. The reference period employed in the two surveys are different. The NWS uses a one-year reference period, and the NCVS a six month reference period. We know that the longer the reference period the greater the under-reporting. Hence, the longer reference period of the NWS should lower rates relative to the NCVS.

CATI. Both the NCVS and the NWS used Computer Assisted Telephone Interviewing (CATI). Only about 30% of NCVS interviews are conducted with CATI while all of the NWS interviews employed CATI. Research on the NCVS indicates that CATI increases the reporting of crimes by about 40% (Hubble and Wilder, 1988), so we would expect that the use of this technology would increase reporting in the NWS relative to the NCVS.

Cuing Strategy. The cuing strategies differ considerably across the two surveys. Both surveys use screener questions to elicit mention of target events and then ask follow-up questions to obtain more information on these events. The screening interview in the NCVS employed a "short cue" strategy for eliciting mentions of candidate events. This approach explicitly acknowledges that respondents may store information in varied ways such that a single question would not be an equally good cue for everyone. Consequently there must be redundancy in cuing so that many cues are given to elicit mention of a particular type of event. This redundancy must, in turn, be accommodated within reasonable limits of respondent burden. Hence the use of a short cue format in which a single syntactically correct question is followed by a large number of short cues. This maximizes the number and types of cues that can be applied and minimizes the time required to administer the cues.

A second concept that guided the development of the new NCVS screener was that of "grey area" events. These events do not subscribe completely to the stereotype of the target event. So, for example, an assault by a sibling may not be considered a crime by a respondent because the offender was not a stranger. The respondent may classify such an attack as a family problem, although similar activity by a stranger would be considered a crime. It is important to instruct the respondent that such events are within the scope of the survey. This was done by explicitly noting with instructions and cues that a "grey area" event should be mentioned. (See Appendix 1).

The NWS survey followed a more traditional cuing strategy where several syntactically correct questions were asked to elicit mentions of rape or attempted rape. The transition statement that preceded the questions on rape included some language that attempted to firm up the grey area of crimes by non-strangers. (See Appendix 1). The density of cues provided in the NCVS was somewhat greater than that offered in the NWS. Strictly on the basis of the number of relevant cues offered, reports of rape and attempted rape should have been higher in the NCVS than in the NWS.

The screening strategy used in the NWS also differed from the NCVS in the explicitness of the language used to cue mentions of rape. The NCVS used the term rape (see Appendix 1). The NWS made explicit reference to the behaviors involved in rape, e.g. "by sex, we mean putting a penis in your vagina." The questions used also make explicit reference to oral, anal, and object sex by force. Not using explicit behavioral descriptions of target events is an aberration in the NCVS. Cuing of other crimes in the NCVS employs explicit reference to behaviors. The explicitness of cues in the NWS should result in higher rates of reporting in that study relative to the NCVS.

Context. The two surveys also vary with respect to the context of the explicit questioning about rape and attempted rape. The principal purpose of the NWS was to identify events and conditions that put respondents at risk of substance abuse. In contrast, the NCVS is designed to identify victims of crime. The purposes of these surveys are explicitly stated and the questions asked prior to the explicit questions about rape clearly imply the focus of the respective surveys. This context can affect the level of rape reported in the surveys. It is possible that the context of traumatic life events will capture more rapes and attempted rapes than the context of crime. This is especially true of grey area events where the circumstances do not conform to our stereotypic notions of crime. The context of crime may inhibit mention of these kinds of events. Respondents may not be willing to mention in a crime survey events where force is ambiguous. They may be less reticent to do so in a survey dealing with traumatic life events. The effect of context is more difficult to predict than the effects of other design attributes discussed here. We know that context is important but we are not yet able to specify the effects on reporting of a particular context.

Series Incidence and Repeat Victimization

The NCVS employs a procedure for handling multiple victimizations that are similar and that the respondent cannot describe separately. Specifically, if a respondent reports more than five events that are similar and indistinguishable, these events will be treated as a series incident. That is, detailed information in the incident form will only be collected on the most recent occurrence of the crime and this incident will be omitted from the annual estimates. This procedure was developed to reduce respondent (and presumably interviewer) burden. It also identifies events for which the Census Bureau felt that the information provided by the informant may not be of very high quality. The attributes of events that are so blurred as to not be distinguishable may not be as accurately reported as events that are more distinct. This suspicion resulted in the omission of series events from annual crime rates. There is no indication in the publicly available documentation of the NWS that a similar procedure was followed for similar events reported in that survey. Presumably, all mentions of rape reported in the NWS were included in the resulting rate estimates. This difference in procedures should make the NCVS rates lower than those of the NWS.

The effects of the foregoing design differences on the estimates from the NWS and the NCVS are summarized in Table 2.

Table 2 Predicted Effect of Design Attributes on Level Estimates
By Study

Design attribute	NCS	NCVS	KILPATRICK
Reference period	Increase	Increase	Decrease
Bounding	Decrease	Decrease	Decrease
Cuing strategy	Decrease	Increase	Increase
Sample attrition	NA	NA	NA
CATI	Decrease	Increase (moderate)	Increase
Context	Decrease	Decrease	Increase
Series procedure	Decrease	Decrease (moderate)	Increase
Population differences	Increase	Increase	Decrease

Many of the hypothesized sources of divergence in the estimates of rape can be tested using data from the NCVS and the NWS. The NCVS data have just been made public as this article goes to press. The NWS data has not been made public and it is not clear when it will be available. It would be useful both for our understanding of rape and our confidence in social statistics that some attempt be made to estimate the magnitude and direction of the effects of design differences on estimates of the incidence and prevalence of rape. Not all of the design differences between the NCVS and the NWS can be investigated through the secondary analyses of the resulting data, but to do so would be a step in the right direction.

Knowing a Good Estimate When We See One

The analysis suggested in the foregoing section may shed some light on the reasons why the NWS and the NCVS produce such wildly different rates for rape and attempted rape. This analysis, however, will not tell us which of the two numbers is more valid. To date in self-report surveys, researchers have assumed that any procedure that gave one more mentions of rapes was better or more valid. Given what we know about retrospective surveys, this is not a bad assumption. Recent advances in screening in retrospective surveys have shown that we have the ability to design screening interviews that will elicit more mentions of potential target events. Adding cues to screening interviews will clearly add incidents to the counts. In light of this, it is conceivable that at some point more may not be better.

This eventuality does not argue for an end to "broad net" screening. Screening interviews should attempt to elicit as many candidate events as possible; otherwise, suspicion of under-reporting will rightfully persist. The potential for over-reporting with "broad net" screeners must be addressed by expanding the information obtained on the incident that is relevant to establishing whether a target event has occurred. In the case of rape more information must be obtained on the crucial issues of consent and force. This additional information can be used to determine if potential events are indeed target events. Events that do not possess the attributes of target events must be treated differently than those that do.

Surveying organizations must also pay much more assiduous attention to this filtering process. Incident forms should be completed for accepted as well as rejected incidents. In this way one can know what is being filtered out in the classification algorithm and what is not. Thereby, differences in the filtering and classification algorithms can be taken into account when alternative designs are evaluated. None of the surveys examined here keep records on the number and nature of events that were deemed ineligible or were classified as some other type of event as a result of questions asked in the incident form.

Crime or incident classifications must also be developed that reflect the broad net nature of screening. In these classifications, provisions must be made for distinguishing between events that are central to the concept and those that are more marginal. So, for example, in the case of rape there should be classes within the broad class of rape that distinguish events in which consent and force are unclear and those in which these issues are extremely clear. The concept of "attempt" that is currently used in rape classifications does not capture the idea of "grey area" events. Assailants can clearly want to affect penetration by force but fail to do so. This would be an attempt. In other cases, consent may be ambiguous so that there is some question as to whether or not the target event has even occurred. These are radically different from attempts and classifications should reflect these differences. Absent these changes in classification, broad net screening will produce the perception of very high rates when the reality may be much lower. The perception comes from treating events that clearly have all the attributes of rape as equal to events in which the present of rape-defining attributes is uncertain. The distinction should be between certain rapes and uncertain rapes in addition to the distinction between attempts and completions.

Greater emphasis on filtering the proceeds of broad net screeners does entail substantial risk. There is broad disagreement on what constitutes rape. It may not be possible to obtain definitions of the bounds of the concept. Even if some consensus is reached on the concept, it may not be possible to design an incident form that could obtain the information required to distinguish between rapes, attempted rapes, uncertain rapes and other events. Moreover, pushing respondent victims on issues of force and consent necessary to make these distinctions increases the chance of refusals and break-offs. Victims may perceive this questioning as blaming the victim. Questioning required for classification may also increase the chance that victims will be hurt by the recalling and recounting required in the interview. All of these outcomes would diminish the ability of self-report surveys to illuminate issues concerning the incidence and prevalence of rape.

Conclusion

The foregoing analyses may shed some light on the reasons why the NWS and the NCVS produce such wildly different rates for rape and attempted rape. Previous work on retrospective surveys (and particularly victimization surveys) offers some plausible hypotheses about why the two designs should yield different estimates of rape. Although the proposed adjustments are crude, they should provide a rough test of some of these hypotheses. Moreover, they offer a test based upon empirical analysis rather than invective. It is important to understand why these estimates differ both for assessing the magnitude of rape and for restoring confidence in self-report measures of crime. Understanding why these self-report measures differ will help to dispel the suspicion that self-report measures are not valid or comprehensible indicators of crime.

The furor over rape and rape statistics highlights the more general and more pressing problem of validating self-report data on criminal victimization. There is no readily available standard for validating these data. Reverse record check (RRC) studies using police reports have been shown to be flawed conceptually and to be extremely difficult (if not impossible) to do well. Comparative studies of different survey procedures (such as that proposed above) are useful alternatives to external data for validation purposes, but these comparisons require assumptions in order to say something about validity. The most common assumption has been that there is more under-reporting than over-reporting in these surveys and that, as a result, "more is better" or more valid. As retrospective surveys appropriately cast broader nets in search of eligible events and screening procedures become more sophisticated (as in the case of the NCVS), the assumption of more is better becomes less tenable. A great deal more attention must be given to the issue of validity in self-report surveys of victimization, so that we are better able to respond when questions are raised about the quality of these data.

Appendix 1

Excerpts from the NCVS and Screener and Incident Forms

NCVS Personal Screening Interview.

30. Before we get to the crime questions, I'd like to ask you about some of YOUR usual activities. We have found that people with different lifestyles may be more or less likely to become victims of crime.

On average during the last 6 months, that is, since _____ _____, 19___, how often have YOU gone shopping? For example, at drug, clothing, grocery, hardware and convenience stores. (Read answer categories until respondent answers yes.)

Mark (X) the first category that applies.

31. (On average, during the last 6 months,) how often have you spent the evening out away from home for work, school or entertainment? (Read answer categories until respondent answers yes.)

Mark (X) the first category that applies.

32. (On average, during the last 6 months,) how often have you ridden public transportation? (Read answer categories until respondent answers yes.)

Do not include school buses.

Mark (X) the first category that applies.

36a. I'm going to read some examples that will give you an idea of the kinds of crimes this study covers.
As I go through them, tell me if any of these happened to you in the last 6 months, that is since _____ _____, 19___.

Was something belonging to YOU stolen, such as –

(a) Things that you carry, like luggage, a wallet, purse, briefcase, book –

(b) Clothing, jewelry, or a calculator –

(c) Bicycle or sports equipment –

(d) Things in your home – like a TV, stereo, or tools –

(e) Things from a vehicle, such as a package, groceries, camera, or cassette tapes –

OR

(f) Did anyone ATTEMPT to steal anything belonging to you?

MARK OR ASK

36b. Did any incidents of this type happen to you?

36c. How many times?

40a. (Other than any incidents already mentioned,) since _____, 19____, were you attacked or threatened OR did you have something stolen from you –

(a) At home including the porch or yard –

(b) At or near a friend's, relative's, or neighbor's home –

(c) At work or school –

(d) In places such as a storage shed or laundry room, a shopping mall, restaurant, bank, or airport –

(e) While riding in any vehicle –

(f) On the street or in a parking lot –

(g) At such places as a party, theater, gym, picnic area, bowling lanes, or while fishing or hunting–

OR

(h) Did anyone ATTEMPT to attack or ATTEMPT to steal anything belonging to you from any of these places?

MARK OR ASK

40b. Did any incidents of this type happen to you?

40c. How many times?

41a. (Other than any incidents already mentioned,) has anyone attacked or threatened you in any of these ways (exclude telephone threats) –

(a) With any weapon, for instance, a gun or knife –

(b) With anything like a baseball bat, frying pan, scissors, or stick –

(c) By something thrown, such as a rock or bottle –

(d) Include any grabbing, punching, or choking –

(e) Any rape, attempted rape or other type of sexual attack –

(f) Any face to face threats —

(g) Any attack or threat or use of force by anyone at all? Please mention it even if you are not certain it was a crime.

MARK OR ASK
41b. Did any incidents of this type happen to you?

41c. How many times?

42a. People often don't think of incidents committed by someone they know . (Other than any incidents already mentioned,) did you have something stolen from you OR were you attacked or threatened by (exclude telephone threats) —

(a) Someone at work or school —

(b) A neighbor or friend —

(c) A relative or family member —

(d) Any other person you've met or known?

MARK OR ASK

42b. Did any incidents of this type happen to you?

42c. How many times?

43a. Incidents involving forced or unwanted sexual acts are often difficult to talk about. (Other than any incidents already mentioned,) have you been forced or coerced to engage in unwanted sexual activity by —

(a) Someone you didn't know before —

(b) A casual acquaintance —

OR

(c) Someone you know well?

MARK OR ASK

43b. Did any incidents of this type happen to you?

43c. How many times?

NCVS Incident Form: Selected Questions.

2. You said that during the last 6 months –
(Refer to appropriate screen question for description of crime.) Did (this/the first) incident happen while you were living here or before you moved to this address?

3. You said that during the last 6 months –
(Refer to appropriate screen question for description of crime.) In what month did (this/the first) incident happen? (Show calendar if necessary. Encourage respondent to give exact month.)

4. If known, mark without asking. If not sure, ASK –

Altogether, how many times did this type of incident happen during the last 6 months?

CHECK ITEM B
Refer to 4.
How many incidents?

CHECK ITEM C
Are these incidents similar to each other in detail, or are they for different types of crime? (If not sure, ask.)

5a. The following questions refer only to the most recent incident.

5b. Was it daylight or dark outside when (this/the most recent) incident happened?

6. About what time did (this/the most recent) incident happen?

....

20a. ASK OR VERIFY
Were you or any other member of this household present when this incident occurred?

20b. ASK OR VERIFY
Which household members were present?

21. ASK OR VERIFY
Did you personally see an offender?

22. Did the offender have a weapon such as a gun or knife, or something to use as a weapon, such as a bottle or wrench?

23. What was the weapon? Anything else?

Mark (X) all that apply.

24. Did the offender hit you, knock you down or actually attack you in any way?

25. Did the offender TRY to attack you?

26. Did the offender THREATEN you with harm in any way?

27. What actually happened? Anything else?

Mark (X) all that apply.

FIELD REPRESENTATIVE – If box 4, ASK –

Do you mean forced or coerced sexual intercourse including attempts?

28a. How did the offender TRY to attack you? Any other way?

28b. How were you threatened? Any other way?

Mark (X) all that apply.

FIELD REPRESENTATIVE – If box 5, ASK –

Do you mean forced or coerced sexual intercourse including attempts?

29. How were you attacked? Any other way?

Mark (X) all that apply.

FIELD REPRESENTATIVE – If raped, ASK –

Do you mean forced or coerced sexual intercourse?

If No, ASK – What do you mean?

If tried to rape, ASK –

Do you mean attempted forced or coerced sexual intercourse?

If No, ASK – What do you mean?

30. Did the offender THREATEN to hurt you before you were actually attacked?

31. What were the injuries you suffered, if any? Anything else?

Mark (X) all that apply.

FIELD REPRESENTATIVE – If raped and box 1 in item 29 in NOT marked, ASK –

Do you mean forced or coerced sexual intercourse?

If No, ASK – What do you mean?

If attempted rape and box 2 in item 29 is NOT marked, ASK —

Do you mean attempted forced or coerced sexual intercourse?

If No, ASK — What do you mean?

Appendix 2

NWS Screening and Incident Description Questions.

Another type of stressful event that many women have experienced is unwanted sexual advances. Women do not always report such experiences to the police or other authorities or discuss them with family or friends. The person making the advances isn't always a stranger, but can be a friend, boyfriend, or even a family member. Such experiences can occur anytime in a woman's life – even as a child. REGARDLESS OF HOW LONG AGO it happened or who made the advances:

48. Has a man or a boy ever made you have sex by using force or threatening to harm you or someone close to you? Just so there is no mistake, by sex we mean putting a penis in your vagina.

49. Has anyone, male or female, ever made you have oral sex by using force or threat of harm? Just so there is no mistake, by oral sex we mean that a man or a boy put his penis in your mouth or someone, male or female, penetrated your vagina or anus with their mouth or tongue.

50. Has anyone ever made you have anal sex by using force or threat of harm? Just so there is no mistake, by anal sex we mean that a man or boy put his penis in your anus.

51. Has anyone, male or female, ever put fingers or objects in your vagina or anus against your will by using force or threats?

52. During your lifetime, how many times (different occasions) have you been forced to have (sex/ oral sex/ anal sex) or been forcibly penetrated with fingers or objects? Please include any incidents that may have happened when you were a child.

53. Did this incident (any of these incidents) occur before you were 18 years old?

54. Did this incident (any of these incidents) occur within the past 12 months or since the last time you were interviewed?

End Notes

1. Koss, Mary. (1992) "Rape on Campus: Facts and Measures." *Planning for Higher Education.* v. 20, Spring, pp. 21-28; Koss, Mary, Gidycz, Christine and Nadine Wisniewski. (1987) "The Scope of Rape: Incidence and Prevalence of Sexual Aggression and Victimization in a National Sample of Women." *Journal of Consulting and Criminal Psychology*, vol. 55, No. 2, pp. 162-170.

2. Young, Cathy. (1995) "Exaggerating the Dangers Women Face." *Detroit News* Mar. 28, A, 9:1; Snow, Tony. (1995) "Pols Play the Numbers Game." *Detroit News*, Mar. 30, A, 15:1; McPhail, Beverly (1995) "The term is 'femicide' and society must do something." *Houston Chronicle*, Oct. 1, C, 4:1; Murray, David. (ND) *America's Phony Rape Epidemic.* Washington, D.C. Statistical Assessment Service.

3. Murray, David. *op. cit.*

4. Gilbert, Neil. (1992) "Realities and Myths of Rape." *Society*, May/June; Koss, Mary. (1993) "Detecting the Scope of Rape: A Review of Prevalence Research Methods." *Journal of Interpersonal Violence*, Vol. 8, No. 2, pp. 198-222.

5. Biderman, Albert D. and James P. Lynch. (1991) *Understanding Crime Incidence Statistics: Why the UCR Diverges from the NCS*, New York, Springer Verlag.

6. Bureau of Justice Statistics. (1992) *Criminal Victimization in the United States, 1990.* Washington, D.C., U.S. Department of Justice; Koss, Mary. (1992) "Rape on Campus: Facts and Measures." *Planning for Higher Education*, v. 20, Spring, pp. 21-28; Ward, Sally K., Kathy Chapman, Ellen Cohn, Susan White and Kirk Williams. (1991) "Acquaintance Rape and the College Social Scene." *Family Relations*, 40: 65-71.

7. This assumption may not be equally appropriate for all subsets of rape. Some argue persuasively that assault victims who are seriously injured are under-represented in self-report surveys of victimization.

8. Biderman, Albert D. and James P. Lynch. (1981) "Recency Bias in Data on Self-Reported Victimization." Proceedings of the American Statistical Association, 1981, Washington, D.C. American Statistical Association, pp. 31-40.

9. Cannell, C.F., Marquis, K.H. and A. Laurent. (1977) "A Summary of Studies of Interviewing Methodologies." *Vital and Health Statistics*, Vol. 2, U.S. Department of Health, Education and Welfare, GPO, Washington, D.C.

10. Koss, Mary P. and M. Harvey. (1987) *The Rape Victim.* Boston: Greene Press.

11. Koss, Mary P. (1993) "Detecting the Scope of Rape: A Review of Prevalence Research Methods." *Journal of Interpersonal Violence*, Vol. 8, No. 2, pp. 198-222.

12. Rand, Michael and Bruce Taylor. (1995) "The National Crime Victimization Survey Redesign: New Understandings of Victimization Dynamics and Measurement." Paper presented at the Annual Meetings of the American Statistical Association, Orlando, FL, August 13-17; Hubble, David. (1995) "The National Crime Victimization Survey Redesign: New Questionnaire and Procedures Development and Phase-In Methodology." Paper presented at the Annual Meetings of the American Statistical Association, Orlando, FL.

13. Series incidents refers to a convention used by the Census Bureau for handling multiple victimization events for which respondents cannot date the individual occurrences. In the old NCS, any respondent who had three incidents of the same type that he or she could not date, could have their experience treated as a series incident. When this occurred the interviewer would record the number of events reported, but collect detailed information only on the most recent event. In the NCVS, the threshold for series incidents was increased three to five incidents. Only multiple victimizations with five or more events can be treated as series incidents.

14. Hubble, David. (1995) *op.cit.*; Persley, Carolyn (1995) "The National Crime Victimization Survey Redesign: Measuring the Impact of New Methods." Paper presented at the Annual Meetings of the American Statistical Association, Orlando, Florida, August 13, 1995.

15. National Victim Center. (1992) *Rape in America: A Report to the Nation.* Arlington, VA National Victim Center.

The Surprising Ease of Changing the Belief That Schools Shortchange Girls

Judith Kleinfeld, Professor of Psychology
University of Alaska Fairbanks

In many university settings, especially Schools of Education, the belief that the schools shortchange girls has attained the status of a religious dogma. This view swept through the media by way of a highly publicized report, *How Schools Shortchange Girls*, published by the prestigious American Association of University Women Educational Foundation together with the Wellesley College Center for Research on Women.

In *Who Stole Feminism?*, Christina Hoff Sommers examines the intellectual shortcomings of this glossy report, intended as an ideological weapon in the gender wars. The AAUW Report, Sommers points out, glosses over inconvenient evidence contrary to their case -- for example, that males are more apt than females to drop out of high school.

Sommers makes a far more serious charge: The AAUW report bases its most dramatic conclusions on a study that has mysteriously disappeared. At issue is widely cited research by David and Myra Sadker claiming to have come up with a shocking finding: Teachers give far more attention to boys, and girls are silenced in the classroom.

The Executive Summary to the AAUW Report, *How Schools Shortchange Girls*, turns this finding into its first and leading point. The opening section, "What the Research Reveals," begins:

What Happens in the Classroom?

Girls receive significantly less attention from classroom teachers than do boys.

The AAUW Report goes on to explain:

> A large body of research indicates that teachers give more classroom attention and more esteem-building encouragement to boys. In a study conducted by Myra and David Sadker, boys in elementary and middle school called out answers eight times more often than girls. When boys called out, teachers listened. But when girls called out, they were told to "raise your hand if you want to speak.

When Sommers tried to locate the original research, she found the study had vanished.

> After exhaustive library and computer searches, I called the Department of Education, which informed me it no longer had a copy. The librarian at the Widener Library at Harvard University did a computer search as thorough and high-tech as any I have ever seen. Finally, she requested it from the Library of Congress. "If they do not have it, no one does," she said, and they did not. In the meantime, one of my undergraduate assistants called David Sadker himself to ask how to find it. He told her that *he* did not have a copy and urged her to have a look at the article in the *Phi Delta Kappan*. We had come full circle.[1]

Furthermore, when Sommers located the article specifically cited in support of the AAUW conclusions, she found that the article focused not on "call-outs" but on reprimands.[2] Boys received eight to ten times as many *reprimands* as did girls. Boys were also more likely than girls to receive public, rather than private, reprimands and more severe penalties.

When I read Sommers' expose, I was horrified. Like many other professors, I routinely covered the Sadkers' research when I discussed gender issues. In a case book I had just published on gender issues,[3] I cited other articles the Sadkers had written on the same theme.[4] If this research did not exist, then I had been unwittingly recruited as a foot soldier in the gender wars.

In my classes, I did present the contrary view -- that males might be the gender shortchanged in the schools. In the 1970s, my students are always surprised to learn, the common wisdom was exactly the reverse. Schools were considered "feminized environments," especially elementary schools. Female teachers, the argument went, preferred female students because they tended to be more responsive to the teachers' directions and had more developed fine motor and verbal skills. Boys were more apt to drop out, to be placed in special education classes, and to have reading disabilities. The policy prescription of that time: Employ more male teachers, especially in elementary schools.

Even though I mentioned this historical change, I gave substantial weight to the Sadkers' "findings." I had spread their message.

As an equity feminist well aware of the problem of politicized research, I was easy to convince. Simple evidence, such as Sommers presented, was enough. Would contemporary college students prove similarly easy to convince? I doubted it.

In discussing gender issues in my classroom, I found that students, both male and female, usually held an intense belief that women were the victims of discrimination. I doubted that such passionate convictions would yield to simple evidence.

Do we accomplish much when we present such rebuttals? Are critics such as

Sommers just preaching to the choir?

I decided to explore the question in my own classroom. Would reading Sommers' rebuttal alter the view that women were discriminated against in the classroom? I didn't think so.

Checking on Sommers' Contention that the Sadkers' Report Had Disappeared. I had been taken in before, and I realized I could be taken in again. Before giving my students Sommers' research, I decided to check her shocking contention -- that this highly publicized report had indeed disappeared.

I decided to call David Sadker directly and ask him for a copy of the lost report. I also wanted to give him the opportunity to answer Sommers' charges. When I telephoned Professor Sadker, he was quite courteous and eager to discuss his own research and Sommers' motivations. But he admitted he had no copy of his own research. He confirmed Sommers' charge -- that this highly publicized and influential research report had disappeared. He referred me to his own university's research office to search for a copy. With such embarrassing charges leveled against his own work, I could not believe that he himself would not have called his own university's research office if the original report could have been obtained with such ease. Since Professor Sadker offered no adequate answer to Sommers' contentions, I proceeded with my own classroom study.

An Exploratory Study

Students. The 61 students enrolled in my required introductory course, "Individual, Society, and Culture," at the University of Alaska Fairbanks are representative of students at a large state university with open enrollment policies. Most students take this course during their first year at the university. The class was equally divided between males (30 students) and females (31 students). While about 15 percent of the students were minorities -- African-Americans, Alaska Natives, and Asian students -- this group was too small to separate out for analysis. Nor did these students, on inspection of their responses, appear to show any pattern of response different from the other students'.

Procedures. On the mid-term exam, as an essay question, I gave students two pages from the AAUW Report[5] highlighting the Sadkers' findings. I then asked this question:

1. Please read the attached excerpt from the report by the American Association of University Women: How Schools Shortchange Girls. Which reaction comes closest to your view?
*a. This research **is convincing**: Teachers do favor males in classroom interactions.*
*b. This research is **not convincing**: Teachers do not favor males in*

classroom interactions.

c.   *I am not sure -- but my opinion is closest to answer a.*

or

c.   *I am not sure -- but my opinion is closest to answer b.*

2.   *Please explain your reaction to this research in **two** or more paragraphs. Why do you find this research convincing or not convincing?*

I followed this question with an excerpt from Sommers challenging the Sadkers' research, followed by a parallel structured question and essay asking them to explain if their views on the matter had changed. Students were told that they would not be graded on the answer they chose but on the quality of their reasoning in the essays.

For clarity of analysis, I grouped the "I am not sure" responses into the categories which the students identified as "closest" to their answers.

Results. On matters where people have a good deal of personal experience, their views are apt to be shaped by their experience, not merely by what "scientific research" says about the question. The issue of whether teachers favor males or females in classrooms is a question where most college students have a great deal of personal experience. As one student put it, "Having been going to school for the past billion years, I'm just as qualified to write about this as the University Women." In view of their own personal experiences and passionate beliefs, I did not expect Sommers' attack on the Sadkers' research to have much of an effect on the students' views. Possibly Sommers'' challenge would give heart to some of the male students who resent feminist charges that they are the "privileged" gender. But many male students, I have found in my own classroom, take strong feminist positions. The basis of their passion seems to be their reluctance to take sole responsibility for the support of a family. They want a society where men and women share this financial burden. Female students, I thought, would be especially ego-involved in the belief that women were discriminated against and even more unlikely to shift their views. Attitudes which serve ego-defensive purposes have been found to be more resistant to change.[6]

I was wrong. To my surprise, both male and female students displayed dramatic attitude change as a result of mere information.[7]

After Reading Sadker. Even after they had read the AAUW selection on the Sadker research arguing that the schools shortchanged girls, students were quite divided in their views. A small majority of students (54%) did agree that teachers favored males (Table 1).

Table 1
After reading the Sadkers' research . . .

Do college students believe that the schools shortchange girls?

	Male	Female	Total
Yes	47%	61%	54%
No	53	39	46
Total	100%	100%	100%
Number	30	31	61

A greater proportion of female students (61%) compared to male students (47%) supported this position. As one young woman wrote:

> After reading the American Association of University Women's report: "How Schools Shortchange Girls," I was not surprised by the findings. As an Elementary Education major with extensive classroom experience, I knew most of the information to be true. The article presented a well-known three year study with well-organized data to back up the report's thesis: Boys are more attended to than girls.

Even though she stated clear agreement, this student retained a skeptical, cautious attitude. She went on to write:

> Despite my initial reaction to the convincing nature of the article, I remain a bit hesitant at the AAU"'s motivation for the printing of such an article and would like to read further into the subject before developing my own final opinion.

Effects of Sommers' Rebuttal: To my surprise, Sommers' rebuttal had a dramatic effect on students' views. After reading Sommers' only a tiny minority -- 6% of the students -- still stated the view that teachers favored males (Table 2).

Table 2

After Reading Sommers' arguments . . .

Do college students still believe that the schools shortchange girls?

	Males	Females	Total
Yes	3%	9%	6%
No	90	68	79
Unclear	7	23	15
Total	100%	100%	100%
Number	30	31	61

The male college students showed a clear and strong shift in attitude with 90% saying that they did not believe teachers discriminated against girls. As one put it:

> This criticism is convincing because it shows people make up facts which are supposed to be from studies, but they do not exist in the study. This shows to me that the person who wrote the controversial article is either misinformed or will lie to get a point across. I believe that when a report needs to falsify information to try and convince people then it should be treated as a fraud and ignored.

While the majority of female students (68%) also found the Sommers rebuttal convincing, a substantial group (23%) responded to the challenge to their earlier position with an ambiguous response. They avoided dealing with the conflict.

To get a clearer picture of which students changed as a result of mere information, I separated the students into two groups -- those who took the initial position that teachers favored males and those who took the initial position that teachers did not discriminate. For those who did not see any teacher discrimination from the start, Sommers' information strengthened and reinforced their original views (Table 3). This was to be expected.

Table 3

Students believing that schools **do not** shortchange girls:

Did these students change their minds?

	Male	Female	Total
Yes	0%	0%	0%
No	94	83	89
Unclear	6	17	11
Total	100%	100%	100%
Number	16	12	28

What I did not expect was the dramatic change among students who first stated that teachers discriminated against girls. Of this group, 70% changed their minds (Table 4).

Table 4

Students believing that schools **do** shortchange girls:

Did these students change their minds?

	Male	Female	Total
Yes	86%	58%	70%
No	7	16	12
Unclear	7	26	18
Total	100%	100%	100%
Number	14	19	33

In short, simple information did result in substantial change in college students' views about whether the schools discriminated against girls. In interpreting the results of this small, exploratory study, it is important to keep in mind that this classroom situation was especially favorable to attitude change for two important reasons. Students were both 1) able and 2) motivated to think through the message. In many situations, persuasive messages are aimed at people who have no interest in scrutinizing them. As Tesser & Shaffer (1990) point out in their review of research on attitude change, "Recipients who are unmotivated or unable to scrutinize message content will adopt opinions that are relatively insensitive to either the quality of message arguments or the character of any issue-relevant thinking."[7]

In this classroom setting, students were highly motivated. Their grades depended on their thinking about the two opposing messages. But this condition underscores an important point: College classrooms are excellent settings to give students the opportunity to consider alternative messages.

Complexity of Students' Views: When I read students' explanations of their views, I was struck by the complexity of their attitudes. Their writing was typical of entering students at an unselective state university -- undeveloped ideas, fragments of arguments, many mechanical errors.

Nonetheless, the students made provocative observations both about differences in the ways boys and girls behaved and teachers' motives for different treatment. They expressed appreciation for the complexity and subtlety of the issues. As one young man wrote in support of the Sadkers' contentions:

> I find this research convincing. Obviously the researchers made a great deal of observations and conducted a great deal of experiments. I believe in the text it read, after several years of research . . . If all the researchers were die-hard Feminists, I can see where some things may be a little misconstrued. Men, as the article said, demand more attention. Some people would argue that this is wrong and should be changed, but I feel this would be as easy as making women grow beards.

A student like this young man is open to evidence, to nuanced ideas, to a discussion of both the cultural and biological influences in male and female development. In the college classroom, we need to offer him not ideology but an education. We need to help him conceptualize the issues, understand the competing political agendas, examine the evidence and then discuss the potential for effective social change. We need to inform and to cultivate the life of the mind.

The Case Approach to Teaching About Gender Issues: To encourage such informed and reasoned discussion about gender issues in the schools, I have developed a series of cases drawn from real-life situations.[8] Modeled after the case approach of the Harvard Business School, each case presents an emotionally-charged dilemma for students to reflect upon. The point is informed analysis of each case, considering such questions as: What happened? What is going on here? Why? What perspectives might other people have? What are the fundamental issues beyond the immediate crisis? What are the possibilities for useful action?

One case, "'Girlspeak' and 'Boyspeak': Gender Differences in Classroom Discussion," raises the issue of gender differences in classroom participation and how teachers might contribute to gender favoritism. The case, based on a real-life situation, presents a social studies teacher struggling to understand the different ways boys and girls talk in his classroom. The teacher asks himself if he could be unintentionally aiding and abetting a situation where he gives most of his attention to a few talkative students, especially one talkative male. The case invites discussion of the bases of these patterns and the extent to which a teacher can or should try to change "girlspeak" and "boyspeak."[9] The case opens the issue of individual, not only group, differences -- some boys do dominate a class but so do some girls, and many students, boys and girls, do not speak at all. The case asks about unintended consequences -- the changes in the quality of discussion in classrooms with prescriptions about who gets speaking turns.

The purpose of this casebook is to present gender issues in the schools -- sexual harassment in the hallways, the lagging of females in math and science classes, the value of classrooms and activities separated by gender -- as matters demanding reasoned and informed discussion. We selected cases which are not morality tales but instead raise troubling issues where reasonable people of good will can disagree.

Conclusion

This exploratory study on whether simple information can change views in the gender wars is limited to one issue, one university classroom, and one fight. Still, the dramatic change in attitude that occurred in college students as a result of mere information is encouraging. Despite the political fervor of the gender wars, students appear to be responsive to evidence. Their attitudes are not hardened. They already hold complex views. By moderating our passions and presenting gender issues as interesting problems rather than as morality plays, we can develop those qualities of mind most conducive to addressing the gender problems that remain with us and appreciating the progress that has occurred.

End Notes

1. Sommers, C.H. (1994). *Who Stole Feminism?* New York: Simon & Schuster.

2. Sadker, D., Sadker, M. and D. Thomas. (1981). "Sex Equity and Special Education." *The Pointer*, 26: 33-38.

3. Kleinfeld, J.S. and S. Yeriam, eds. (1995). *Gender Tales: Tensions in the Schools.* New

York: St. Martins Press.

4. Sadker, D. and M. Sadker (1985a). "Is the Ok Classroom Ok?" *Phi Delta Kappan*, 55: 358-367; Sadker, D. and M. Sadker (1985b). "Sexism in the Schoolroom in the '80s." *Psychology Today*, 19: 54-57.

5. American Association of University Women (1992). *How Schools Shortchange Girls: Executive Summary*. Washington, D.C.: AAUW Educational Foundation, pp. 68-69.

6. Tesser, A. and D.R. Shaffer. (1990). "Attitude and Attitude Change." *Annual Review of Psychology*, 41: 479-523.

7. I present these tables without statistical test of significance. Since these students constitute a "population" rather than a "sample," statistical tests would be inappropriate.

8. Tesser, A. and D.R. Shaffer. (1990). *op. cit.*

9. An accompanying teacher's manual offers teaching suggestions and references to research and other literature to help teachers' discussion in ways that illuminate the complexities of these issues and add informed perspectives to the discussion.

Heterophobia: The Feminists Turn Against Men

Daphne Patai, Professor
Department of Spanish and Portuguese,
University of Massachusetts at Amherst

Something very strange happened toward the end of the twentieth century. Women turned against men. Lives of human complexity, filled with both affection and antagonism, slowly began to be perceived as intolerable, perhaps despicable. Even someone like Simone de Beauvoir, formerly seen as a feminist heroine, a fighter for women's rights, became suspect because of her attachment and dedication to Jean-Paul Sartre. Intellectual companionship and lifelong love and friendship were now recast as subservience.

To take another example, heterosexual intercourse got reclassified as "rape" and women's power to "consent" was dismissed as powerlessness to resist patriarchal impositions. Heterosexual women had to be wary of revealing conflicts in their personal lives, since any such admission seemed to carry the expectation that they would ditch those men at once and set out on their own.

Heterosexuality -- this is what I am saying -- went from being the norm to being on the defensive. I call this phenomenon *heterophobia* -- the fear of difference, fear of the "other." I am using the term heterophobia to refer specifically to the feminist turn against men and heterosexuality. Of course, the attitudes I have been describing are not held by *all* women, not even, perhaps, by *many* women, though certainly they are found among many feminist women. Nor am I saying that heterophobia is the work of lesbians, since they, vastly outnumbered by heterosexual women, could never have succeeded in imposing such an agenda had it not been acceptable to heterosexual feminists as well. But if homophobia is still a problem in the society at large, heterophobia is feminism's own predictable reversal of that problem.

Heterophobia is by no means an entirely new phenomenon, though never has it gone so far or gained such notoriety as in the past couple of decades. When Mona Caird in the 1880s agitated against marriage, or when Cristabel Pankhurst published *The Great Scourge* in 1913 and described men as repulsive carriers of venereal disease, these women were combating particular social conditions. Their attacks were often immoderate, and there is in first wave feminism a strong and well-known anti-sex aspect. Some women engaged in purity campaigns and argued for chastity, for both men and women; they opposed legalization of prostitution; some called for censorship of written materials and of art work depicting nudity. They judged male politicians on the basis of sexual morality, as did Lucy Stone in opposing Grover Cleveland's candidacy in the presidential election of 1884 because he had supposedly fathered -- and taken responsibility for -- an illegitimate child. All of these things, in other words, are familiar.

But one thing we can say about these 19th- and early 20th-century women: they emphatically did not support any sort of double standard, whereby homosexual sex was to be encouraged and promoted, while only heterosex was seen as corrupting and contemptible. In a historical moment in which women were struggling to win basic political rights -- and resting their claims on arguments that they had the *same* intellectual and moral capacities as men -- heterophobia would clearly not be a winning tactic. The relative restraint of most early feminists is even surprising, for a more aggressive stance certainly could have been justified. Doesn't it make sense to deplore women's relationships with men at a time when those relationships are characterized above all by women's civic inequality, their extreme economic dependence, lack of education, vulnerability to constant pregnancy and its attendant dangers -- that is, increasing pauperization, ill health, death?

We in this country -- feminist scare statistics to the contrary -- hardly live in that sort of world. Most (though not all) women today have many options, due above all to their access to education and to birth control and their resulting position in the labor market. And perhaps precisely because of these shifts, which have enormously increased women's autonomy and life opportunities, heterophobes wishing to attack men must find ever new and more dramatic grounds for doing so.

In working on a book on the phenomenon of heterophobia, I am particularly interested in how heterosexual feminists experience being both feminist and heterosexual at a time when the two categories are often presented as antithetical, and when hetero women's sexual preferences and experiences are being redefined and debased by rather silly but nonetheless influential ideas put forth in the name of feminism.

What, for example, is a heterosexual woman to do in a climate that tells her that male potency is a threat? That the penis is an instrument of domination? How many hetero feminists fail to challenge heterophobia out of a secret belief that only lesbian feminists are The Real Thing? How common is it for heterosexual women who call themselves "feminists" to find their heterosexuality complicated by their feminism? How productive are such tensions? Do they lead to inhibition and awkwardness as the "heterosexual body" comes under postmodernist scrutiny? How do women negotiate the ensuing problems? How do they compare any difficulties they encounter with the gains they feel they have made because of feminism? How frequently are they turned off feminism, or cease to relate to the term? And, a very important question, how much of a role do such matters play in "ordinary" women's alienation from feminism? This alienation, in my view, is by no means a result of "backlash" or bad public relations, but a legitimate perception of much feminist discourse.

It seems to me crucial to distinguish between hating the sin and hating the sinner (to use a Christian metaphor). But somewhere along the line the criticism of patriarchal institutions derailed into a real, visceral, and frightening antagonism toward men and a consequent intolerance toward women who insist on associating with them. I'm amazed, as I think about it, that hetero women have knuckled under to this stigmatizing of their sexual desires and personal relations -- but without question many of them have done so. Let me give you a few examples.

While interviewing students for the book (co-authored with Noretta Koertge)

Professing Feminism: Cautionary Tales from the Strange World of Women's Studies (BasicBooks, 1994), I was told by a women's studies major that the teacher of one of her courses kept referring to her "partner," without ever using any pronoun. The class assumed the teacher was a lesbian, and this student was shocked -- and felt deceived -- when she accidentally discovered that the teacher was heterosexual, married, and had a child. My question is: Why does a teacher feel obliged to engage in such a cover-up?

Another example, small but telling: after one of my early articles criticizing feminist excesses, I received a letter from a male professor who told me that he and his wife, also a professor, had been very active in setting up a women's center on their campus. When it came time to celebrate the center's anniversary, his wife had asked him not go to the event, saying: "I don't want to flaunt my heterosexuality." And I myself, I must admit, have taught lesbian utopian novels in my courses on women's utopian fiction without ever uttering a word of criticism that their visions offered no hope for heterosexual women.

How heterophobia works out at the level of social behavior is often bizarre: I remember a meeting of some women faculty members who got together weekly for lunch, at Indiana University where I was on leave in the mid-80s. One day one of the members of the group announced she was going to be married. There was an absolute dead silence in the room. Obviously we feminists were far too sophisticated to shriek and express happiness, and no one knew what to do as an alternative. So, stunned silence for far too long greeted her announcement. (She did, incidentally, redeem herself by getting quickly divorced a couple of years later.) I have no doubt that if her announcement had been that she'd fallen in love with a woman and was about to move in with her, the reaction would have been quite different.

It seems to me that much of the present passionate rejection of men is explained, only apparently paradoxically, by feminism's embrace of "difference." There are so many groups to which any one group of feminists need feel inferior: white women vis-a-vis women of color; hetero women vis-a-vis lesbians; well-off women vis-a-vis poor ones (though, characteristically in American society, this theme is of less importance than the others). The fact is that feminism is fragmented by all these divisions, which have created something that, in our book *Professing Feminism*, Noretta Koertge and I referred to as the "oppression sweepstakes." I believe this jostling for place creates so much tension within feminism that it is barely able to sustain itself as a movement in which separate identity groups keep speaking to one another. But there is *one* thing that, apparently, can save the day for them all, and that is hostility to men.

I think, then, that the crude attack on men as a group provides some psychological ballast to feminists otherwise pulled in different directions by the highly politicized atmosphere in which we live. One lesbian I know deplores the heterophobic trend within feminism and has written to me in disgust that this amounts to casting men as what she calls "the universal scapegoat." Of course, on reflection, this label, too, requires further qualification, since women of color and women from other parts of the world at times argue that their struggle is "together with" their men. From my observations, however, the white women who swallow such talk don't really like it, and only racial identity politics keeps them from directly challenging it. So it is white men who are indisputably at the pinnacle of the hated heap -- as dishonest as this is since, of course, significant social divisions and highly variable behavior exist among white males as within any other group.

No one acquainted with women's studies programs or feminist circles generally will deny that some of the most widely taught and read figures are the notorious heterophobes Catharine MacKinnon, Andrea Dworkin, and Mary Daly. I will not, in my comments, call these women "radical" feminists, as they are so often labeled, because I do not believe they go to the "root" of anything. Instead, I believe they manifest a pathological aversion to men, and I hold that their views have had a strong and negative influence on feminism and its future, in the classroom and out.

One might, of course, argue that extreme positions such as "all intercourse is rape" or "all men are potential rapists" are useful as catalysts for social change, calling attention to the demand that rape should *never* happen, that *no* woman should ever be the victim of sexual assault. And I think, in fact, that something must be conceded to such an argument. But it's by no means the whole story. How can one view with equanimity a world in which women feel free to make grossly demeaning generalizations about half the world? Consider the following examples:
Last year, on FEMISA, an e-mail list devoted to issues of gender and international relations, someone wrote that she was preparing a paper arguing that fathers are necessary for children's development. But, she said, "I would be helped by arguments that proved the opposite: that men are unnecessary for a child to grow into mature adulthood." Quite a few people were happy to oblige. One wrote:

> Men, as a group, tend to be abusive, either verbally, sexually or emotionally. There are always the exceptions, but they are few and far between (I am married to one of them). There are different levels of violence and abuse and individual men buy into this system by varying degrees. But the male power structure always remains intact.

Another poster wrote a long message in the same vein:

> Considering the nature and pervasiveness of men's violence, I would say that without question, children are better off being raised without the presence of men. Assaults on women and children are mostly perpetrated by men whom they are supposed to love and trust: fathers, brothers, uncles, grandfathers, step-fathers.

Disregarding the ample evidence of child abuse initiated by women, this message continued:

> I agree with the many feminists who have argued that the role of fathers

as perpetrators of sexual, emotional, and physical violence against female children is absolutely critical to the maintenance of male supremacy. Through incest, girls learn about subordination on the most basic level, and are thus prepared for their proper roles as women in this society.

Men who do not fit this profile are so few as to be "negligible." In a stunning example of concept stretching, this last contributor explained that when she uses the word "abusive," she means "to include the assertion of male dominance." Though FEMISA as a list is supposed to maintain an "international" perspective, these posters did not even bother to qualify their statements, which presumably were intended to characterize all males in all countries of the world. Such words are not considered "flames" but perfectly appropriate messages, and when some men on FEMISA *did* protest the male-bashing on the list, they got tossed off the list.

When I hear such mind-numbing caricatures of behavior on which, alas, males have no monopoly, I am often reminded of a scene I repeatedly witnessed years ago when I was living in Paris. At the post office, at the end of the week, working-class men who were obviously immigrant laborers in France (Greek and Turkish men mostly, at that time) used to line up to send their money home, often to places so remote that long discussions ensued as the post office clerks tried to figure out just which particular town or island was intended. I used to stand in line behind these men, week after week, asking myself: what keeps them coming back here? Badly dressed, surely living in poor accommodations, yet faithful, determined to send money home, how do they do it? Nothing in the feminist extremist vision allows one to understand the behavior of such men -- except, of course, the gross supposition that they're merely manifesting their economic power so that one day they can go home and resume beating up their wives and children.

At about the same time that I was mulling over the behavior of these men, a woman in the United States published what became a famous "feminist" document. She wrote:

> Life in this society being, at best, an utter bore and no aspect of society being at all relevant to women, there remains to civic-minded, responsible, thrill-seeking females only to overthrow the government, eliminate the money system, institute complete automation, and destroy the male sex.[1]

This statement comes from Valerie Solanas, whom some may remember as the author, in the late 1960s, of the SCUM manifesto. By being SCUM -- members of the Society for Cutting Up Men -- Solanas argued, women could quickly take over the country. Foreshadowing the intense animosity between many feminist women and their non-feminist sisters, she pinpointed the real conflict as not that between females and males, but between SCUM -- whom she defines as women who are dominant, secure, proud, independent, and so on -- and those she contemptuously labels "approval-seeking Daddy's Girls" (516). Among the things SCUM will do when it takes over is "destroy all useless and harmful objects -- cars, store windows, 'Great Art,' etc." (517). "SCUM will couple-bust," she ominously announced; it will "barge into mixed (male-female) couples, wherever they are, and bust them up."

And, in case anyone is in some doubt as to what SCUM has in mind for men, Solanas spells it out (showing that Mary Daly and Andrea Dworkin are mere late-comers and also-rans): "SCUM will kill all men who are not in the Men's Auxiliary of SCUM. Men in the Men's Auxiliary are those men who are working diligently to eliminate themselves" (517).

Solanas can probably be dismissed as part of the lunatic fringe. She is, after all, the woman who, in 1968, shot and nearly killed Andy Warhol over his apparent lack of interest in a film script she had submitted to him.[2] But what shall we make of Sally Miller Gearhart, a professor of communications who, nearly fifteen years after Solanas, wrote an essay entitled "The Future -- If There Is One -- Is Female,"[3] in which she argues that the future must be in female hands, that women alone must control the reproduction of the species (with men given no say in it whatsoever), and that only 10% of the population be allowed to be male? Gearhart plays a few notes of sweet reason, saying that we can't be sure that men are inherently destructive or women naturally nurturing. This is why, she admits in all seriousness, she has not suggested that men be eliminated altogether.

Like Gearhart, I myself used to believe that women should run the world -- since even if we couldn't be sure what women *would* do, it was reasonable to believe we would make no worse a job of it than men had done. That was before I spent years in a women's studies program, and saw for myself how, in practice, women deal with conflict, an experience which convinced me that women are not superior to men in political virtue, kindness, or even plain good sense, and that persuaded me that we should keep muddling on toward equality between the sexes, doing our best to avoid the language of hate.

But this is not what feminist extremists have in mind. Like Valerie Solanas and her SCUM manifesto, Professor Gearhart calls upon men to participate in their own demise by voluntarily helping in reducing their own numbers (she makes reassuringly clear that she does not contemplate mass murder, but, rather, slow attrition through new reproductive technologies and voluntary support from men for feminist goals). And from what I see on the feminist e-mail lists, there are groveling males in the world who would go along even with this for the sake of maintaining their status as "feminist men." It appears that not only women are inclined to knuckle under to strong speech and intimations of power.

Gearhart's essay on the female future in fact reveals that in her view not all women are equally qualified to construct the better society to come. One would, of course, want to know up front how conflicts among women are to be resolved in Gearhart's vision. It appears, alas, that she has nothing to say about this. But as a lesbian-feminist activist, she does know *which* women can be permitted to exercise power. Women who might not go along with her views are, she says, "enslaved by male-identification and years of practice within the system" (270). In short, no attention need be paid to them. Such women, along with men, will need to be subjected to "education" in the "voluntary [sic] and vast changes that must take place."

The idea that women's rule would necessarily lead to peace and order (a staple of feminist utopian fiction, a subject I have been teaching for years), and that political in-fighting would vanish is, of course, nonsense. It is a childish dream, perhaps a touching dream, but still merely that. Let us ignore, for the moment, the fact that women as a group are not united by identical ideas (how could they be?); women are not, after all, natural socialists, as many feminist writers like to pretend. What do we find when we actually observe how women handle conflicts? One woman, Rachel Bedard, who became a lesbian separatist for a while after her marriage failed, has left this account:

> I moved into a separatist house with tremendous expectations of feminist support and nurturance. But within weeks we were divided over everything from dinner hour to cats to who owned which soap in the bathroom. [4]

No doubt feminist extremists can blame this, too, on The Patriarchy. In any event, the household broke up, and eventually, though ostracized by feminist friends for doing so, this woman returned to heterosexuality. She titled her account of these experiences "Re-entering Complexity." If even a self-selected group within one small household encounters such problems, imagine what would happen in a world run by women.

Shall we trust our feminist leaders in the future to "somehow" make peace between groups as divided as pro-choice and anti-choice women? Between those that want conventional religion in the schools and those that will allow none -- or perhaps only Goddess worship? Can anyone genuinely believe that conflicts would not continue?

If we reject -- as it seems to me obvious we must -- the notion that women would create a world of eternally peaceful sameness, we have the right, even the obligation, to ask what sorts of political processes feminists will set in place. And how will the feminist future deal with dissenters? Perhaps feminist utopian fiction has something to say on this subject. Alas, it all too rarely does. Even my undergraduate students notice that Charlotte Perkins Gilman's utopian novel *Herland* (1915), which describes an all-female society, *presumes* lack of conflict rather than outlines mechanisms for dealing with it; and they notice, too, the coercive manipulations which subtly underlie that society: the pressure brought to bear on women who are not -- by the society's eugenic standards -- deemed worthy of reproduction (accomplished, in the novel, through parthenogenesis). And if social pressure fails, the novel tells us, more stringent measures are taken. These measures, however, are *not* described in the novel, so we are left to wonder: perhaps the uncooperative women undergo forced abortions?

Recalling many feminist utopian novels, in which there is little individual autonomy, the anti-sex rhetoric (and, more generally, the anti-male campaign) of contemporary heterophobes is an intense assault on the private sphere. And it makes sense that extremists should go after this sphere, for it is in the realm of the personal that their ideas are most vulnerable. After all, the vast majority of women *are* heterosexual and do want relationships with men. Attempting to "bust up" male-female couples, as Valerie Solanas put it, is thus an indispensable first step. But for lesbian women, too, this assault should be of concern, since it is designed to cut them off from male friends, children, brothers.

Not surprisingly, perhaps, feminist extremists at times exempt themselves from the behavioral norms they wish to impose on all other women. In practice, they often carve out little pockets in which *their* particular personal lives and tastes can continue untainted, and it is only *other* women whose lives need to be scrutinized, regulated, and -- if they do not measure up -- scorned. How else explain that Andrea Dworkin, with her notoriously hateful writings about men and heterosex in general, has also written lovingly about her own father, a feminist man to whom she says she owes her passion for writing and her independent spirit? How else explain Catharine MacKinnon's apparent belief that while *other* women cannot give informed consent, she herself can? This seems a fair inference to draw from those affectionate photographs seen a few years ago of MacKinnon arm-in-arm with her then-fiancé Jeffrey Masson. Clearly, these women are prepared to impose their views on others, while, for themselves, they maintain the rights belonging to autonomous adults. This is the standard tactic of authoritarian leaders.

Faced with the incontrovertible fact that many women who *are* economically independent seem to like living with men, heterophobes have had to bring out the heavy artillery. (I will not devote time to their intellectually reprehensible love of inflamed statistics.) The older of the two main tactics is simply to unleash the language of hate against men, to heap such scorn on them that it becomes difficult for self-respecting women who consider themselves feminists to associate with men. This is the approach that is encapsulated in such phrases as "sleeping with the enemy."

The second, and newer, technique, is the postmodernist obfuscation that "problematizes" not only gender but also sex, and represents these as entirely imaginary constructs which, once we see through the fraud -- or, rather, through the "social construction" of these categories -- will liberate us. In other words, once we learn that "sexual preference" and even one's own "sexual identity" are misnomers for social conditioning, forcing us to select our lovers from only a particular group of people, heterosexual relations as we know them, along with all questions of "identity" and "preference," will come to an end. For in this view, not only gender but even sexual identity is performance, it is ideology, but it is certainly not an essential part of the self-definition of free and thoughtful human beings who actually are born female and male.

On one feminist e-mail list last year a professor wrote in excitedly that she was teaching her students that all sexual identity -- our identity as males or females -- is a social construction. She cited research such as that of Anne Fausto-Sterling, who has written that as many as four percent of neonates are born as hermaphrodites and are surgically forced to conform to either male or female bodies.[5] Postmodern feminists are happy to extrapolate from such research that the other 96% of us, too, have not only gender roles but actual sexual identity forced onto us, and that a less patriarchal society would encompass many many sexes.

Though fun to play with in theory, such ideas in practice seem designed not so much to add fascinating diversity to the already hectic human scene but rather, quite specifically, to dissolve the maleness of men and heterosexual women's attraction to it, never the femaleness of women-loving-women.

Now, some of the reasons for advancing these arguments are easy to understand. Perhaps some folks think it is possible to gain civil equality for gays and lesbians only by stigmatizing heterosexuality, or at least by "problematizing" it. In this view, feminism and gay-rights activism are zero-sum games: whatever I win, you lose. If my being homosexual is to be valued, your being heterosexual must be despised. This, of course, seems a doomed strategy, since such theorizing will have little effect on the vast majority of the population, who will no doubt go right on being obnoxiously heterosexual while experiencing nothing but alienation from feminists who tell them they shouldn't be doing what they're doing, and certainly should not consider it "natural!"

"Problematizing sexuality" is what we find done, for example, in a recent article in the *National Women's Studies Association Journal*, which argues that a partner's sex should be no more significant than any other personal characteristic that makes us prefer one individual over another.[6] I doubt that such sophisticated postmodernist theorizing will be successful in permanently separating women from men. In fact, I have often wondered why, given the failure to wipe out homosexuality even in truly repressive and homophobic times, we should believe that redefining heterosexuality as "compulsory," as Adrienne Rich does in her famous essay, would cure anyone of it.

Another dismal example of postmodernist approaches to sexuality -- and a sublime instance of heterophobia -- is provided by a recent article entitled "The Medicalization of Impotence: Normalizing Phallocentrism," by Lenore Tiefer. Its abstract states this:

> Today, phallocentrism is perpetuated by a flourishing medical construction that focuses exclusively on penile erections as the essence of men's sexual function and satisfaction. This article describes how this medicalization is promoted by urologists, medical industries, mass media, and various entrepreneurs [offering treatments for impotence]. Many men and women provide a ready audience for this construction because of masculine ideology and gender socialization.[7]

In this view, nobody really needs an erect penis. Presumably, the author of this article would prefer to live in the world of Professor Sally Gearhart's feminist utopia *The Wanderground*, where the women's only male allies (of whom they're nonetheless suspicious) are the gay men, called "gentles," who have voluntarily accepted impotence. In other words, the only good man is an impotent man.

Am I making too much of an admittedly minority position within feminism? Am I arguing against all common sense that heterophobes are taking over and that men will soon be in danger of extermination? Either physically wiped out or simply *thought* out of existence? No, I would not want to go nearly that far. But I am saying that the language of hate, which is prevalent in feminist writings, *should* be taken seriously. It is no more acceptable in the mouths of women than in the mouths of men, no more tolerable coming from so-called radical feminists than from the Ku Klux Klan.

But surely, one might retort, there really isn't much cause for alarm. Heterophobes today don't have state or even local power. They're not in a position to enforce their ideas. In one sense, this is of course true. But let's look at the kinds of power feminist ideas *have* achieved. The relations between men and women have indeed become -- as theorists love to say with approval -- "problematized." So much so that any word, any gesture, may these days give offense to women. If in the old days women's complaints against men's abusive behavior were seldom taken seriously, today they are given if not automatic credence, at least the benefit of the doubt. Nor is this just a matter of social norms, of casual office behavior. There are men who have lost their jobs -- certainly in academe, which is the area I know best -- because of flimsy allegations of sexual harassment. Men are being deprived of due process. And many feminists quite explicitly and seriously consider that this is the way things *should* be. Due process, in their view, is nothing more than one of the patriarchy's power tools, just like freedom of speech.

Feminism has in fact been remarkably successful in creating a climate in which men's words and gestures are suspect, and in which it is now women's charges that are given quick credibility. Tell an innocent man who has lost his job in a university, and cannot get another one, because of a charge of sexual harassment, that feminists don't have power. But, of course, it is not only men who are the victims of such accusations. Women in academe, too, though much more rarely, are being accused of "sexual harassment" -- I put the phrase in quotation marks because some of these charges are quite ludicrous -- when it suits the agenda of others, even of so-called feminists. Still, this inconvenience should not obscure the fact that it is men who are the intended targets of the brave new heterosex-free world extolled by many feminists.

It is frightening to see a society unleash against its own citizens codes of speech and behavior that can ensnare just about anyone, and that have as their rational underpinning nothing more than a woman's sense of "discomfort" around certain phrases or deeds. To conflate this with serious acts of sexual harassment and abuse is to invite totalitarianism -- the heavy hand of authority everywhere in the private sphere, until there is virtually no private sphere left. Is this an enactment of the feminist vision? It sounds more like the dystopias we're all familiar with from the novels of Zamiatin and Orwell, in which there is a close correspondence between political control of sexuality and the creation of an atmosphere of hysteria that has as its aim the suppression of the private sphere and the redirecting of individuals' energy toward state goals and definitions.

Consider, as well, the truly bizarre and frightening climate surrounding child sexual abuse and "recovered memories" as they are called. Innocent people are in prison as I speak because of so-called "evidence" that any sane society would have laughed out of court. Tell those victims that feminist ideas about the protections we all need from the demon of sexuality have not had any effect. Or consider the case of "visual harassment" -- as one Minneapolis construction supervisor called it when urging his crew not to look at women passers-by.[8] Perhaps all men should keep their eyes on the ground, the strategy once adopted by Black men in the American South to protect themselves from charges of giving offense to white women. And what about the absurd suspicion that massive sexual harassment is going on in schoolyards, and the demand of grown women that little boys be made to face up to it and reform?

All these examples, I think, show that women's revenge is no longer just a fantasy. True, heterophobes do not yet have the political power to make everyone shape up, but the writings of the most notorious and least responsible among them have enormously contributed to the creation of a climate in which individual autonomy and its sexual manifestations in particular are under attack. And what is the justification for this state of affairs? It's all supposedly done for "our own good," and such niceties as democratic process and first amendment rights may just have to be sacrificed.

It is to protest this state of affairs that I am doing research on the phenomenon of heterophobia. Heterophobia should not be mistaken for a sentimental return to Victorianism. On the contrary, it seems to me that what is going on today fits right in with the dismaying history of twentieth-century totalitarianisms. This tendency toward totalizing pronouncements, this absence of respect for the political process -- the essence of which, after all, is compromise -- is quite blatant among feminist extremists. But we all bear responsibility for it if we do not speak out against it. Heterosexual women must stop acting apologetic or embarrassed about their attachments to men, must stop, in other words, accepting the ideological framework set out by heterophobes, which turns the phrase "heterosexual feminist" into an embarrassing oxymoron. Lesbians, as well, must make it clear that to be a lesbian is not to be a man-hater by protesting the work of those lesbian writers who seek to make the two synonymous. Men too must speak up for themselves and against the indignities and falsehoods that feminist rhetoric heaps upon them as a group -- a tactic that, these days, would never be tolerated if it were directed against, say, Blacks, or Hispanics, or Jews, or women as a group. It is absurd to characterize every man who won't agree with feminist positions as a throwback who is, by his very disagreement, demonstrating the male drive to dominance and the desire to keep women barefoot and pregnant.

To my mind, it is astonishing that decades of progress for women, decades of denunciation of misogynist ideas, should have brought us to the point where a mere reversal -- misandry instead of misogyny -- should count as serious feminist thought and should be taught and promoted in the name of feminism. Thus the historical spectacle of sex antagonism continues, with no hope that it will ever be superseded. And, ironically, feminists thereby prove that they are no different from their masculinist counterparts.

But though it's not difficult to match crazed feminist proclamations of our time with crazed masculinist ones from the past, there are two important differences:

The first is that aside from collections of misogynistic rants across the centuries -- the sorts of things professors like to hand out to their students to shock them into sudden awareness of male disdain for women and the need to combat it on all fronts -- few people today are exposed to persistent hysterical denigrations of women. Whereas, of course, there does seem to be a large and apparently insatiable market for the writings of feminist extremists, and their authors are without question among the best-known names in contemporary feminism.

The second difference is that no one has ever believed that the old misogynistic rantings could pave the way toward a better future, whereas somehow heterophobes have gained credence for many of their ideas, which are often defended precisely in the name of some ideal female future. Why should we not, then, hold feminists to the high standards they themselves profess when they denounce their masculinist predecessors?

I seem to be arguing, on the one hand, that feminist extremism has brought about very negative results -- such as the exorbitant sexualization of all interactions between men and women, the vigilante mentality, the vocabulary of sexual harassment even at the kindergarten level, the denial of due process in universities and the work place to men accused of sexual misdeeds, the attack on the rights of fathers, and so on.

On the other hand, I am suggesting that this sort of feminism is doomed to failure because it alienates many women -- and, of course, men, too. So which is it? Has heterophobia been successful or is it doomed to failure? The two views can, I think, be reconciled. We need to acknowledge that the negative consequences are real, and are being felt -- in unjust and frivolous accusations against men (and against women too), in the resulting loss of reputation and even of livelihood, in a strained atmosphere between the sexes, in assaults on freedom of expression and association. But all these are short term results, so clearly leading to a worse world that they can't possibly endure. Other, more tyrannical and much more powerful ideologies have self-destructed; so will this. And when that happens, the damage done to feminism in the eyes of millions of potential supporters will be clearly felt, for the feminism that aimed at promoting justice and equality, not anger and revenge, will have been tainted as a far-out movement, represented by the male-bashers (who are indeed often the loudest among feminist spokespersons), and enormous effort will be required to restore feminism to the dignity it deserves.

Because feminist extremism is creating a well-earned bad name for itself, and because it is genuinely harming people, women and men who want a better society must speak out against it, and they must do so, I think, without allying themselves with reactionary forces that truly do desire to see women under men's thumbs once again.

There have always, of course, been sane feminists, who have seen the dangers of the domination of either sex over the other. One such figure was the British writer Katharine Burdekin, who, in the 1930s, wrote a series of remarkable feminist-inspired utopian and dystopian novels. In a novel called *Proud Man*, originally published in 1934, Burdekin outlined her critique of a world run by women. The narrator of the novel, an androgynous being from a future that it calls *human*, observes life in England in the 1930s and comments on the behavior of us *subhumans*, still living in "the childhood age." This is what the narrator says:

> If women retain their biological importance, and become pleased with themselves from birth, and learn to associate power with the womb instead of with the phallus, a dominance of females over males is not only possible but likely. Their self-confidence, which would be rooted as deep as the old male jealousy, would cause in them a tremendous release of psychic power with which the males would be unable to cope. Naturally a female dominance would make the race no happier, nor bring it a whit nearer to humanity. The privilege would merely be reversed, and possibly it would be more oppressive and more cruel.[9]

Twenty years ago I would never have suspected that we, today, would need to hear such a warning. The lack of political power that heterophobes have at the moment should not deceive us about the kind of world they clearly want to bring about -- and would if they ever gained the means to implement their designs. As I have argued throughout this essay, their success in introducing an element of genuine paranoia into the relationships of ordinary men and women should not be taken lightly. It should be revealed for what it is: a project posing as utopian that would in fact be a nightmare.

End Notes

1. Solanis, Valerie [sic], "Excerpts from the SCUM (Society for Cutting Up Men) Manifesto," in *Sisterhood is Powerful*, ed. Robin Morgan (New York: Random House, 1970), p. 514.
2. Bockris, V. *The Life and Death of Andy Warhol* (New York: Bantam, 1989). Infuriated by Warhol's apparent rejection of a film script entitled "Up Your Ass," which she had submitted to him, Solanas hounded Warhol for months, finally confronting him on June 3, 1968 in his office and shooting and nearly killing Warhol and wounding one of his associates (pp. 222-236). On June 13, Solanas appeared in court accompanied by two representatives of NOW, Ti-Grace Atkinson and the attorney Florence Kennedy. Atkinson said of this court appearance that Solanas would go down in history as "the first outstanding champion of women's rights," and Kennedy called her "one of the most important spokeswomen of the feminist movement" (p. 236). Solanas was indicted for attempted murder, declared incompetent to stand trial, committed to a mental institution, and then, in June 1969, sentenced to three years for "reckless assault with intent to harm" (pp. 245-248). She died in 1988, and recently became the subject of a film directed by Mary Harron, entitled "I Shot Andy Warhol." It is interesting that the preliminary reviews (e.g., by Janet Maslin, in the *New York Times*, April 5, 1996) are not alarmed at Solanas's violence but treat her as a free spirit and celebrate this in the movie. One can well imagine the reaction if a male would-be murderer were celebrated this way on film.

3. In *Reweaving the Web of Life: Feminism and Nonviolence*, ed. Pam McAllister (Philadelphia: New Society Publishers, 1982), pp. 267-284.

4. Bedard, R. "Re-entering Complexity," in Pam McAllister, ed., p. 401.

5. Fausto-Sterling, A. "How Many Sexes Are There?" *New York Times*, March 12, 1993, p. A29(L).

6. Stearns, D.C. "Gendered Sexuality: The Privileging of Sex and Gender in Sexual Orientation," *NWSA Journal*, Spring 1995 (7:1).

7. *Gender and Society*, September 1994. My thanks to Cathy Young for this example.

8. See, for example, Wayne Washington, "No Eyeful, So City Gets an Earful," *Star-Tribune Newspaper of Minneapolis*, August 5, 1995, p. 1A.

9. Burdekin, K. [Murray Constantine], *Proud Man*. Foreword and Afterword by Daphne Patai. New York: The Feminist Press, 1993 (orig. pub. 1934), p. 31.

Jungle Red: Clare Boothe Luce and the Spirit of the Women's Freedom Network

Laurie Morrow, Professor
Department of English, Louisiana State University, Shreveport

Hollywood, the head cheerleader of political correctness, is about to do something startling. According to *Entertainment Weekly*, *Murphy Brown* creator Diane English has scripted the remake of a classic movie famous for its juicy female roles. Shooting will begin late in 1996, with a $40 million budget. In a preproduction meeting, some of today's most bankable actresses -- including Julia Roberts, Meg Ryan, Candace Bergen, and Marisa Tomei -- gathered for a read-through for Sony Studios.[1] As they did nearly half a century ago for the original film, actresses are hotly competing for even the minor roles.

Business as usual? Permit me to explain: the classic being remade is MGM's *The Women* (1939), a movie as politically incorrect with respect to feminism as it is possible to be. What's going on here, and what has any of this to do with the Women's Freedom Network?

Clare Boothe Luce's *The Women*

The Women started out as a Broadway hit comedy by Clare Boothe (who would later marry *Time* magazine mogul Henry Luce). Despite the play's all-female cast, *The Women* attracted large audiences of both sexes and, consequently, the attention of Hollywood. Anita Loos did the screenplay adaptation, maintaining Boothe's acidic satire while transforming her risqué humor into more marketable family fare. Loos retained the all-female cast of the stage production (a wiser approach than that used in the 1956 musical remake, *The Opposite Sex*, starring June Allyson). Although the women characters speculate at length about the thoughts and actions of the men in their lives, the only on screen image of a man is a silent shadow at the end.

P.C. feminists, one would think, would find the plot of *The Women* thoroughly off-putting. Devoted wife, mother, and homemaker (already we're in trouble) Mary Haines, played by Norma Shearer, spends much of her time with her female friends, an assortment of various female types linked by a common delight in gossip. Foremost among the gossip mongers is Sylvia Fowler, played by Rosalind Russell, in the first of her many effective comic roles. Fowler is a woman who never heard a nasty rumor she didn't delight in and immediately pass along. Thanks to her friends' gossiping, Mary learns that her husband is having an affair with salesgirl/gold-digger Crystal Allen, brought to scheming life by Joan Crawford. Discontent with their own lives, and envious of Mary's loving marriage and family life, Mary's friends enjoy increasing her pain and further injuring her pride by passing along gossip about her errant husband, helping convince her that divorce is her only option. Mary's mother, however, counsels her distraught daughter that even the finest men have flaws, and that part of commitment means having faith that your mate will rise above his weaknesses. Above all, her mother warns Mary to avoid confiding in her girlfriends, as they will try to destroy her marriage for sport.

Mary, her pride injured and, thanks to her chums, inflamed, dismisses her mother's advice as old-fashioned self-abnegation and insists on seeking the "support" of her friends, who do precisely what her mother predicted. Though her penitent husband apologizes and repeatedly begs for reconciliation, Mary, egged on by her friends, insists that reconciliation is impossible, goes to Reno, and files for divorce. Surrounded by a pack of disgruntled divorcées-to-be at a ranch in Reno waiting out the legal time limit to obtain a divorce, Mary eventually realizes what she stands to lose, and how much of her loss is due to the malicious influence of her buddies. Unfortunately, before she can call off the divorce proceedings, her husband calls to tell her he's marrying Crystal.

After Mary has a falling out with Sylvia, Mary's friends quickly discard her and spitefully transfer their affections to Crystal, who has become the new Mrs. Haines. Mary learns from her daughter of Crystal's mistreatment of her ex-husband and of his misery in his new marriage, and decides to reclaim her husband. Now aware of the Rules of Engagement when dealing with unprincipled, manipulative women, she paints her fingernails a predatory shade called "Jungle Red" and dons her slinkiest outfit for a carefully planned encounter with her husband and, more importantly, with her former female friends, whom she tricks into exposing Crystal's infidelities. As her false friends had used her pride to manipulate her, Mary now uses their duplicity and indiscretion to expose their true natures and regain her husband.

What made *The Women* a Broadway hit and a film classic were its satiric sketches of flawed female types, machine-gun-paced humor, effective, albeit soapy, plot, and incisive wit. The satire is most keenly directed at the way women sometimes depend too much on the solace of unctuous female chums, who often, for recreational purposes, maliciously encourage the problems concerning which they are supposedly comforting their friend. Such false friends thrill at the prospect of torpedoing other women's marriages for the chance to make a more dramatic contribution to the gossip. They also clinically enjoy experimenting in the craft of making others more unhappy than themselves. A wise woman, in Boothe's world, learns to measure in precise thimblefuls how much she can trust her female friends.

Enter P.C. Feminism

Given *The Women*'s deft and unrelenting attack on women, this movie would seem an unlikely choice for a Hollywood remake. *The Women* attacks female friendship, a favorite sacred cow of many current "chick flicks," and champions a woman who focuses her energy not on breaking any glass ceilings but on recapturing her ex-husband and restoring her happy family life. *The Women*'s vision of women runs counter to the teachings of politically correct feminism. Back in the '70s, feminism was supposed to change the manner in which women related to their world and to each other. They would go out into the workforce, where they would find greater fulfillment than in traditional female roles. In both the public and private arenas, women, rather than undermining each other as rivals for men, would be mutually nurturing sisters.

But a funny thing happened on the way to sisterhood. Instead of remaining confined to the private sphere -- to the sort of domestic-oriented gossip and backbiting we see in *The Women* -- intrasex antagonism became ideological as well as personal. Women who had the temerity to disagree with any aspect of the feminist agenda -- women who were reluctant to relegate child-rearing to daycare, who considered affirmative action patronizing, who insisted their husbands, brothers, fathers, and sons were basically decent men -- were branded gender traitors. Especially unwelcome was humor, particularly humor directed at any "sister's" ideas, however goofy. Wit and irony, like logical reasoning, were dismissed as evil, intimidating constructs of the oppressive patriarchy. Balloons full of hot air need to be carefully protected from well-pointed barbs of wit.

Even now, some twenty years after feminism hit full steam, p.c. organizations concerned with "women's issues" (a sexist term, implying that men do not care about such things as childrearing, family violence, or equal opportunity) remain humorless gatherings of the grimly earnest and drably dressed. Concealed under a veneer of professed caring is a diligence in repressing freedom of speech and thought that makes Joseph Stalin look like Thomas Jefferson. No matter what degrees the members hold nor what tolerant sentiments they profess, the p.c. women's organization is no place for the lively exchange of ideas. Humor directed at women, except against women with right-of-center politics, remains *verboten*, for p.c. feminists know that humor is a demonstration of power: when we laugh at someone, we demonstrate the limitation of her power over us. As they crave power over others' words, deeds, and thoughts, p.c. feminists rankle at humor, for it betrays an independence of spirit they despise.

There are some women of intelligence, however, who enjoy a good laugh and a lively argument. The Women's Freedom Network is an organization of such well-balanced, dare one say "empowered," women. It is a women's forum in which logic reigns over feelings, facts over impressions, courtesy over passion. Drawing its membership from across the political, religious, racial, and social spectrum, the organization has no ideological litmus test. Unlike most women's groups, the WFN welcomes genuine diversity of opinion on even the most controversial of issues. Because WFN members recognize that "women's issues" are of concern to both sexes, men, too, are welcome members (approximately 25% of the membership is male). Members are bound together by a common commitment to several principles: to the belief that truth is best sought through reasoned discourse; that, as Rita Simon eloquently argues, facts, even when unpleasant, matter; and that ideas should be communicated in an atmosphere of civility.

Clare Boothe Luce: A Kindred Spirit

In *The Women* Clare Boothe Luce attacks her foolish female characters as strongly as she does because she recognizes that women are capable of being much better people than they sometimes choose to be -- much more loyal, more discreet, more compassionate. None of her characters, even those who suffer most and most elicit our sympathy, is a true victim of anyone save herself. *The Women* shows that we must be detached and objective when pondering the faults and virtues of our own sex as well as when we tally up the sins of the opposite. Like Mrs. Luce, the Women's Freedom Network expects a lot from women. This organization does not see women as hapless victims but as able to solve their own and their society's problems through their execution of personal responsibility, integrity, courage, and character. At last October's meeting in Washington, D.C., for example, former U.N. ambassador Jeane J. Kirkpatrick traveled through torrential rain to deliver a moving, yet also often wryly witty, discussion of past attempts by the United Nations to improve women's treatment in cultures which are genuinely repressive. Court TV reporter and attorney Ricki Klieman traced the relationship between media exposure and justice in the most famous family violence trial of our time -- the O. J. Simpson murder case. Cathy Young's presentation on sexual harassment and discrimination law called for a reduction in the vagueness in which these issues are often shrouded. Through humor, Tama Starr, CEO of a construction company, illuminated the absurdities of affirmative action documentation requirements by displaying the three-inch stack of government-mandated paperwork that a contractor must nimbly maneuver through to fulfill a simple, two-page contract.

Whither *The Women*?

Just what the makers of the most recent version of *The Women* intend remains to be seen. The spirit of the original film is comical and satirical, but the informing muse of today's p.c. feminists is tragic and clumsily didactic, with every woman a victimized Antigone oppressed by a lunkheaded Creon, and every audience a bunch of monkeys who must be taught to see, hear and speak ill of the patriarchy on every possible occasion. It seems doubtful that Diane English, the p.c. Muse of *Murphy Brown*, will produce a movie that attacks the whole concept of sisterhood, presents women as catty rivals down to their taste in embroidered towels, and champions loyalty to a husband who proves less than perfect. The casting of Julia Roberts, best known for playing a hooker in *Pretty Woman*, as the super-innocent Mary Haines suggests a reconception of the role, as does casting Meg Ryan as Sylvia. That something very different from the original is being conjured is suggested by Jane Fonda, of all people, being seriously considered for Mary Haines's wise mother.

It seems likely that the characters will be distorted beyond recognition according to the tenets of feminist political correctness. Will Sylvia's treacherous gossip be linked to verbal abuse in childhood by her sexist father and brothers? Will Crystal seek treatment for sex addiction? Will Mary win her hubby back and then demonstrate her new power and self-esteem by dumping him on her own terms? Will the scratching cats be reconciled and share a group hug?

By the end of this year, when this new movie is due to begin filming, we should have a better idea of how the original screenplay will be reinvented. But perhaps I'm wrong: perhaps Hollywood's p.c. feminists have developed a new enthusiasm for women with traditional goals and values. Perhaps they feel a new respect for traditional marriage and a new understanding of the difficult concessions that must be made to maintain relationships. Perhaps they now reject the unqualified glorification of female friendships. Perhaps I'm the Queen of Romania.

End Notes

1. Natale, Richards. "Petticoat Junction: Meg Ryan and Julia Roberts Fire Up the Remake of 'The Women.'" *Entertainment Weekly*, 28 June-5 July, 1996, pp. 8-9.

Index

Note: Page references followed by *t*, *f*, or *n*, indicate tables, figures, or notes, respectively